KU-289-429

Mathematics Activities for Elementary School Teachers

A Problem Solving Approach

Dan Dolan
Mathematics Supervisor
Montana Office of Public Instruction

Jim Williamson
Visiting Instructor
Montana State University

The Benjamin/Cummings Publishing Company, Inc.
Redwood City, California · Fort Collins, Colorado ·
Menlo Park, California · Reading, Massachusetts · New York ·
Don Mills, Ontario · Wokingham, U.K. · Amsterdam ·
Bonn · Sydney · Singapore · Tokyo · Madrid · San Juan

Sponsoring Editor: Lisa Moller
Editing and Design: Larry Olsen
Cover Design: Vicki Philp

Copyright © 1990 by The Benjamin|Cummings Publishing Company, Inc. All
rights reserved. No part of this publication may be reproduced, stored in a retrieval
system, or transmitted, in any form or by any means, electronic, mechanical,
photocopying, recording, or otherwise, without the prior written permission of the
publisher. Printed in the United States of America. Published simultaneously in
Canada.

Cover image reprinted from GAMES Magazine, copyright © 1983
PSC Games Limited Partnership

Library of Congress Cataloging-in-Publication Data
Dolan, Dan.
    Mathematics activities for elementary school teachers : a problem
 solving approach / Dan Dolan, Jim Williamson.
       p.   cm.
    ISBN 0-8053-0392-8
    1. Mathematics—Study and teaching (Elementary)   2. Problem
solving.   I. Williamson, Jim.   II. Title.
 QA135.5.D64   1990
 372.7'2—dc20   89-18106
               CIP

ISBN 0-8053-0392-8

BCDEFGHIJ- AL - 9 3210

The Benjamin/Cummings Publishing Company, Inc.
390 Bridge Parkway
Suite 102
Redwood City, California 94065

PREFACE

ABOUT THIS BOOK

Mathematics Activities for Elementary School Teachers offers a hands-on, problem solving approach to learning and teaching elementary mathematics. The activities in this book correspond to the chapter titles and topics in *Mathematics for Elementary School Teachers*, Fourth Edition, by Rick Billstein, Shlomo Libeskind, and Johnny Lott (Benjamin/Cummings, 1990). Although this book is designed to supplement that textbook, it can also be used to develop students' understanding of mathematics concepts in three different settings:

- mathematics content courses for preservice elementary teachers, grades K–8
- mathematics methods courses for preservice elementary teachers, grades K–8
- inservice courses and staff development workshops for elementary and middle school teachers

The activities in this book demonstrate an alternative approach to the usual teaching and learning of mathematics. Each activity may be used to:

- develop a mathematical concept
- reinforce a concept that has been previously taught
- illustrate applications of mathematical concepts in contextual situations

Although the laboratory activities are designed for preservice and inservice classes, each one contains suggestions for adapting the activity for use with elementary students at various grade levels, K through 8.

A NEW APPROACH

In *Everybody Counts: A Report to the Nation on the Future of Mathematics Education* (Mathematical Sciences Education Board, 1989), it states: "Those who would teach mathematics need to learn contemporary mathematics appropriate to the grades they will teach, in a style consistent with the way in which they will be expected to teach. . . . The content of the special mathematics courses for prospective elementary and middle school teachers must be infused with examples of mathematics in the world that the child sees (sports, architecture, house, and home), examples that illustrate change, quantity, shape, chance, and dimension."

Both *Everybody Counts* and *The Curriculum and Evaluation Standards for School Mathematics* (National Council of Teachers of Mathematics, 1989) describe knowing mathematics as having the ability to use it in meaningful ways. In the process of learning mathematics, teachers must do mathematics—investigate, conjecture, discuss, and validate—in order to develop confidence in their own mathematical ability and to instill an appreciation of its value in their students.

These mathematics reform documents call for a basic restructuring of the mathematics curriculum beginning at kindergarten. This restructuring affects both the mathematics content of the elementary curriculum and the instructional practices of teachers. As stated in the NCTM *Standards*, "To equip students for productive lives in the Information Age, the definition of success in mathematics— the objective of mathematics—must be transformed." This transformation necessitates dramatic changes in the ways teachers learn and teach mathematics. Alternative methods must be presented to preservice and inservice teachers so that they can learn and practice them while they are in the learning process themselves.

GOALS OF THE BOOK

This book involves preservice and inservice teachers in doing mathematics rather than simply reading about mathematics. It is not intended to be a textbook for a mathematics content course at the college level or to provide all the mathematical content necessary for such a course. This resource book is intended to be used as a companion to textbooks such as *Mathematics for Elementary School Teachers,* Fourth Edition, to involve elementary teachers in discovering mathematical concepts, doing real problem solving, and exploring mathematical concepts in interesting and stimulating settings. By learning concepts through a problem solving activity approach, by developing ideas from the concrete level to the abstract level, and by connecting multiple representations of mathematical ideas, students will gain a broader and deeper understanding of mathematics and will begin to construct their own meanings of mathematical concepts.

Everybody Counts and the NCTM *Standards* advocate that students should:

- become mathematical problem solvers
- learn to communicate mathematically
- learn to reason mathematically
- become confident in their ability to do mathematics
- learn to value mathematics

These goals are consciously reflected in the activities in this book. All the activities have been tested extensively with teachers in inservice programs and with elementary students. The activities have proven effective and stimulating with both groups. We hope that those who use this book will enjoy exploring mathematics, will become confident in their ability to do mathematics, and will come to love it as we do.

INTRODUCTION

CONTENT

This book contains 54 laboratory activities designed to provide preservice and inservice teachers with opportunities to explore mathematical ideas using a problem solving approach and a variety of manipulative materials. For the most part, the activities do not require expensive or single-use materials, yet we have purposely included some commercial manipulatives that can be used at many levels and in a variety of settings. This problem solving approach can enhance the development, reinforcement, and application of mathematical concepts in a way that practicing rote skills cannot. It also engages teachers in a way of learning mathematics that we hope they will apply to their elementary students.

Each activity in this book contains worksheets that students can complete (these pages can be duplicated for use with elementary students at a later time). Preceding each activity is a detailed instructional plan to help the instructor and students to derive the fullest benefit from the activity.

Some activities include a Looking Back section that extends the scope of the activity. These problems require the student to identify the problem solving strategies used in the activity, to do the activity using a different strategy, to relate problems to similar problems, or to discuss or develop extensions of the activity. Answers to the problems appear at the end of the book.

INSTRUCTIONAL SETTINGS

MATHEMATICS LABORATORY   In the mathematics laboratory, students should complete the activity in groups of two to four. The instructor or a lab aide is responsible for discussing the objectives and directing the activity. Once the activity has been completed, the instructor reviews and extends the activity by facilitating class discussion of the results, summarizing the activity, and formalizing the mathematical content. This may include suggestions for adapting the activity for use in an elementary classroom. This instruction should focus on the problems associated with using the activity with elementary students, the importance of the activity in the mathematical development of elementary students, the different approaches that could be used for various grade levels, and the modifications necessary for different instructional objectives, such as developing a concept or reinforcing a concept previously taught.

INDEPENDENT USE   Students may also work independently, or preferably with a small group of classmates, without assistance from an instructor. Students should complete the activity pages as if they were being done in a laboratory setting. Groups of students should discuss the problems and instructional plans as they proceed through the material. During the next regular class period, the instructor should review and extend the activities as described above.

If no summary is provided by an instructor, students can review the Key Ideas and Extensions sections accompanying each activity to confirm their results and to determine whether they have investigated all the related concepts and applications.

Although the activities may be completed independently, we have assumed that students will be working in a laboratory setting or cooperatively outside class. We designed the activities to encourage cooperative learning and to enhance communication about mathematics.

TIME REQUIREMENT

It may appear that these activities will demand a great deal of class time. However, these activities can replace much of the lecture time that is usually devoted to teaching some topics. Many concepts are developed in the activities by working from the concrete level to the abstract level. Through a carefully guided discussion of the results of an activity, students will develop their own mental constructs of the concepts being presented.

ORGANIZATION

The instructional pages, which precede the student pages for each activity, include the following elements:

- **PURPOSE** outlines the major mathematical concepts that are developed in the activities and describes which of the three major objectives—developing, reinforcing, or applying a concept—the activity is designed to meet. For quick reference, this information is also summarized in the Skills Chart on page xiii.
- **MATERIALS** describes any special equipment or supplies that are needed for each activity. We assume that each student will have copies of the activity pages, so these pages have not been listed as needed materials. Some pages that are specially formatted for use with the activities are included at the end of the book.
- **REQUIRED BACKGROUND** explains the prerequisite skills students should have or concepts students should know to successfully complete the activity. We assume that these are part of the students' background or that they have been taught as part of the course.
- **TIME REQUIREMENT** provides an indication of the time needed to complete and discuss each activity. The times are estimates based on the authors' use of the activities in preservice and inservice classes. The total time needed to complete an activity may vary considerably, depending on how thoroughly the points in the Key Ideas and Extensions sections are explained and discussed.
- **GETTING STARTED** explains any preparation necessary before using the activity, suggests previous activities that may be used to develop the prerequisite background, and provides ideas for introducing and motivating the activity. Several sections include more than one student activity. In these cases, it is not always essential to do all the activities. GETTING STARTED explains the sequence in which the activities should be completed and indicates which ones may be used independently of the others.

  Since the purpose of these activities is not just to teach mathematical concepts but also to illustrate how the concepts should be taught to elementary students, it is important that students keep the following questions in mind and formulate answers to them as they are completing each activity:

  - How could this activity be used with elementary students?
  - At which grade level would the activity be appropriate?
  - Could the activity be used at more than one grade level?
  - What adaptations would be necessary to make the activity useable with elementary students at various grade levels?
  - How would this activity be important to the mathematical development of elementary students?

- **KEY IDEAS** summarizes the major concepts of the activity and provides specific points for the class discussion. These suggestions are not a comprehensive list of all the possible concepts that may be discussed; in many cases, only a brief description of an idea is presented, and it is left to the instructor to elaborate on the concepts and develop other points.

- **EXTENSIONS** presents many suggestions and ideas for extending the activity to other mathematical topics or making connections between the mathematical concepts in the activity and their application in the real world or in other curricular areas. Included are some or all of the following:

    - Additional questions and problems to explore
    - Suggestions for using technology
    - Questions to extend ideas in selected problems or the entire activity
    - Sources of other activities, problems, and information related to the concepts in the activity

    The purpose of these questions is to illustrate the Looking Back stage in George Polya's problem solving model. Several activities also include a Looking Back section specifically designed to accomplish this purpose.

- **IN THE CLASSROOM** includes ideas about how each activity may be adapted for use with elementary students. Many activities can be adapted to several grade levels by using only part of the activity or by eliminating more difficult problems.

    The course instructor should read the Key Ideas and Extensions sections carefully prior to using the activity with a class. The major points and questions contained in these sections should be included in the class discussion or assigned as additional investigations.

    Students doing an activity independently should first complete the activity and then carefully review these two sections to derive maximum benefit from the suggestions. Later, when using the activity with elementary students, elementary teachers should follow the suggestions to the course instructor in the previous paragraph.

ACKNOWLEDGMENTS

We would like to thank the following people for helping us to develop this book:

- To Rick Billstein, Shlomo Libeskind, and Johnny Lott for asking us to write these activities and for their encouragement and assistance as we wrote them.

- To Lisa Moller and Mary Ann Telatnik, editors for Benjamin/Cummings Publishing Company, for guiding the manuscript through to publication.

- To Larry Olsen, editor and designer, for his outstanding work in editing the manuscript and the artistic design of the copy.

- To Maurice Burke, Montana State University; Don Collins, Sam Houston State University; Gilbert Cuevas, University of Miami; William Doyle, Bethel College; Mary Lindquist, Columbus College; and Jim Trudnowski, Carroll College, for their reviews of the text. Very special thanks to Mary Lindquist, who went far beyond the usual review process and offered many ideas and suggestions to improve the material.

- To the students of Maurice Burke, Glenn Allinger, and Lyle Andersen at Montana State University, and Jim Trudnowski at University of Montana, for pilot testing some of the activities and for their suggestions and criticisms, which have been included in the revisions.

- To the many students and teachers who have been in our classes over the years for their patience, understanding, critical evaluations, and many ideas that have guided us in writing activities such as these.

- To Houghton Mifflin Company for permission to use the data from the *1987 Information Please Almanac*, edited by Otto Johnson, copyright 1986.

CONTENTS

ABOUT THE AUTHORS

DAN DOLAN Dan Dolan has been the State Mathematics and Computer Education Supervisor in the Montana State Office of Public Instruction for the past eight years. Prior to that, he taught middle grades and high school mathematics for twenty years. He also teaches mathematics education courses at the university level. While teaching in Columbus, Montana, he codirected a nationally validated curriculum development project entitled *Math Lab Curriculum for Junior High School*. He has authored numerous articles, coauthored three books, presented inservice workshops and conference sessions at meetings throughout the country, and served as an editorial consultant for four textbook companies. Most recently, he was a member of the 5–8 writing group, which developed the *Curriculum and Evaluation Standards for School Mathematics* for the National Council of Teachers of Mathematics.

JIM WILLIAMSON Jim Williamson is presently a Visiting Instructor of Mathematics at Montana State University. Prior to that, he served as the Mathematics Specialist for the Billings (Montana) public schools. He has been involved in mathematics education for twenty years and has taught mathematics at all levels from fourth grade through college. He was awarded a Presidential Award for Excellence in Mathematics Teaching in 1984. While teaching in Columbus, Montana, he codirected *Math Lab Curriculum for Junior High School*. He has authored several articles, coauthored one book, and presented inservice workshops and conference sessions at meetings throughout the country. He has served on the NCTM committee that developed tests and coaching materials for the MATHCOUNTS competitions. He chaired the committee for the 1989 competition and served as chairman of the MATHCOUNTS Calculator Pilot Project.

SKILLS CHART

D = develops concept
R = reinforces concept
A = applies concept

CONTENT AREA		Number Patterns	Logical Reasoning	Attributes	Loops	A Visit to Fouria	Largest and Smallest	Target Number	Charged Particles	Integer Patterns	The Square Experiment	Interesting Numbers	Pool Factors	Square Fraction	People Proportions	Population Studies	Patterns in Repeating Decimals	Flex-It	Target Number Revisited	Monte Carlo Simulations	What's the Average?	Statistics With "M&M's"®	The Weather Report	Classify Triangles/Quadrilaterals	Triangle Properties	Art and Geometry	Outdoor Geometry	Motion Geometry	Pick's Theorem	Right or Not?	Mysterious Midpoints	Rectangles and Curves
DECIMALS	x and +						R							A	A				A													
FRACTIONS	concept													D																		
	conversion to decimals													A	A	A																
	operations													R																		
GEOMETRY	congruence			D										R										D	R		R					
	similarity			D										R										D	R	A						
	Pythagorean Theorem																												D			
	figure identification		R	R										R										A	R					R	R	
	properties of figures																							D	D		A		D	A		
	transformations																											D				
	perimeter																												R			A
	area													R													R		D	R	A	
	coordinates and graphing																						A		A				A		A	A
	measurement														A		A			A		A		A	A	A	A	A	D	A		
INTEGERS	concept								D																							
	operations	A							D	D																						
NUMBER THEORY	primes and composites										D	R	A	A																		
	prime factorization											R		A																		
	complete factorization											R	R	A																		
	place value					D	R																									
	LCM and GCD												A																			
PERCENT	concept																					A										
	percent increase														R		R															
PROBABILITY	counting principles		D								R			R																		
	concept																			R												
	simulations																			D												
RATIO AND PROPORTION	concept														D	R	R		R							A	A					
	application														A	D	A				A				A	A	A			A		
REASONING	direct	A	D	D	D		A	A			D					D				A	A				R			R			A	A
	indirect		D		D		A				D														R							
	conjecture and validate	D	R	R		R	A		R	A	A	A		R		A			A		R			R	R	A			A	R	R	A
SETS	concept			D	D		A		A																							
	operations			D						R																						
STATISTICS	mean, median, and mode															A					D	R	A									
	bar graphs / line graphs																					A	D	A								A
	box and whisker plots																						R									
	stem-leaf plots																						R									
	sampling																					D										
WHOLE NOS.	operations	A				R	R	R																								
PROBLEM SOLVING	patterns	D		A	A		A		A	A	A	A	A		A		A												A			
	guess and check		A	A	A		A	A				A	A							A												
	elimination		D	A	A		A																									
	simplify						A					R	A						R										A			
	make a model					A			A		A		A	A					A	A						A		A	A	A	A	A
	make a list or table	A	A	A	A	A			A	A	A	A		A	A	A	A		A					A	A	A	A			A	A	A
	sorting and classifying		A	D	D		A	A	A				R											R	A					R	A	
	estimation / mental math						R	R									R		R													

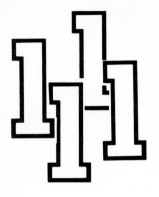

PROBLEM SOLVING

ACTIVITIES:
I. NUMBER PATTERNS
II. LOGICAL REASONING

I. NUMBER PATTERNS

PURPOSE

This activity introduces the pattern problem solving strategy and develops the relationship between the terms of a sequence and the term number. It also develops a procedure for determining a function (rule) that describes a linear sequence of numbers.

REQUIRED BACKGROUND

Students should:

- be able to identify the pattern in a sequence of numbers and determine additional terms in order to extend it
- understand the use of variables in order to generate a function (rule) to describe a linear sequence

TIME REQUIREMENT

- Making Sequences and Constant Differences: 50 to 60 minutes
- What's the Rule?: 20 to 30 minutes outside of class

GETTING STARTED

The Making Sequences and Constant Differences pages can be completed together with little instruction. Emphasize the difference between the *term number* and the *term* itself. Students should understand that *term numbers* are natural numbers and that each *term* in a sequence is determined by some rule. Review the Key Ideas for these two activities before assigning What's the Rule?.

KEY IDEAS

MAKING SEQUENCES Discussion of the first set of problems should focus on the pattern and the method to be used to complete the sequence. It is important to emphasize that just knowing a few initial terms in a sequence is not sufficient for determining a unique function to describe the sequence.

For example, consider the sequence beginning with the terms 1, 2, 4, ... It is possible to conclude that the sequence is :

A. 1, 2, 4, 7, 11, 16, . . . $\dfrac{n^2 - n + 2}{2}$

B. 1, 2, 4, 8, 16, 32, . . . 2^{n-1}

C. 1, 2, 4, 8, 15, 26, . . . $\dfrac{n^3 - 3n^2 + 8n}{6}$

If one were given five terms, such as 1, 2, 4, 8, 16, . . . , one might conclude that the sequence is the same as sequence B, or

1, 2, 4, 8, 16, 31, . . . $\dfrac{n^4 - 6n^3 + 23n^2 - 18n + 24}{24}$

However, regardless of the number of initial terms given, more than one
sequence may be possible. The given terms may be the result of some
function. However, a formal proof is required to show that the function
works for *all* cases.

   While reviewing problems 6 through 9, discussion should focus on these
key points:

A. If the rule involves multiplying the *term number* by a constant, the
    difference between successive terms is that constant. For example, in
    problem 6,

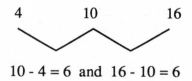

4   10   16

10 - 4 = 6 and 16 - 10 = 6

   Therefore, the constant multiplier is 6.

B. If the constant multiplier is a negative number, as in problem 7, the
    sequence is *decreasing*.

C. When the difference between the successive terms is *not constant,* as
    in problems 8 and 9, the rule does not involve multiplying the *term
    number* by a constant.

CONSTANT DIFFERENCES and **WHAT'S THE RULE?** The following important points should be emphasized during class discussion:

A. Each *term* in the sequence is determined by applying some rule to the
    term number. Stress the fact that, on the Making Sequences page, the
    rules containing a constant multiplier result in sequences with a
    constant difference between successive terms. Also emphasize that
    whether the constant multiplier is positive or negative determines
    whether the sequence is increasing or decreasing.

B. Students should explore the problem of generating the 50th, 150th, or
    1000th term by adding the constant difference. Although this approach
    may solve the problem, students need to learn that it is inefficient,
    time consuming, and prone to error.

C. Once the constant difference has been determined and the term
numbers have been multiplied by it, the key to discovering the rule
for the sequence is in the What Was Done? column. The What Was
Done? question simply asks, what did we do to the multiples of the
constant difference to get the terms in the given sequence?

D. Since the second sequence on the Constant Differences page is decreasing, the constant multiplier is negative. The previous steps can be
followed exactly to determine the function and any term.

These points are simple and can be easily applied to determine a rule that
describes a linear sequence. It should be emphasized that this method
works only for linear functions, those sequences where the difference
between the successive terms is a constant. Although the method can be
generalized to higher order functions, other steps are necessary for it to be
applied.

EXTENSIONS

MAKING SEQUENCES As an assignment related to problems 5 through 9,
have students make up their own rules for generating a sequence and list
the first few terms. Suggest that they develop increasing and decreasing
sequences with constant factors and sequences in which the difference
between successive terms is not a constant.

When they have completed this assignment, have some students describe
their rules and have others generate the appropriate terms. This group
activity helps to reinforce the distinction between *term* and *term number*.

CONSTANT DIFFERENCES and WHAT'S THE RULE? The process that is
illustrated on the Constant Differences page for generating a function that
describes a linear sequence can be generalized to higher order functions.
As previously shown, when the difference between successive terms is a
constant, the function will be linear, or first degree. When the second
order differences are constant, then the function will be quadratic, or
second degree. For example:

Sequence		2		5		10		17		26. . .
First order differences			3		5		7		9	
Second order differences				2		2		2		

The function will be of the form $Ax^2 + Bx + C$, and

$$A = \frac{Constant\ Difference}{2!} = \frac{2}{2!}$$

When the third order differences are constant, the function will be of the
form $Ax^3 + Bx^2 + Cx + D$, and

$$A = \frac{Constant\ Difference}{3!}$$

In general, the degree of the function is equal to the number of differences necessary to determine a constant difference. If A is the leading
coefficient of the function, then

$$A = \frac{Constant\ Difference}{n!}$$

where n is the number of differences.

The extension of this method (and those described in publications on finite differences) provides alternative procedures, such as solving systems of simultaneous linear equations, for generating functions of degree greater than one.

IN THE CLASSROOM

MAKING SEQUENCES With the exception of problems 7 through 9, this activity can be used in grades 4 and up. Students in these grades should explore many problems like these. However, the problems should be consistent with the students' grade level.

In the primary grades, students should be given many experiences with patterns. Building trains with colored blocks or rods, constructing geometric patterns with various sized and colored shapes, and skip counting are various ways to involve children with patterns.

Skip counting should be explored often with primary students as an introduction to multiplication. While lining up to enter or leave the classroom before or after school, at lunch time, or at recess, students can be given a rule and a beginning number and asked to skip count by twos, threes, fives, and so on. After many such experiences, students can be assigned counting numbers according to their position in line or their seats in a row in the classroom. Following skip counting (by threes, for example), students can explore the relationship between their position in line (the assigned number) and the number they said when counting. That is, the third student said "nine," the fifth student said "fifteen," and so on. Activities such as these provide an excellent introduction to mutiplication, the use of ordered pairs (3,9), (5, 15), and elementary notions of relations and functions in addition to developing concepts of patterns.

CONSTANT DIFFERENCES and WHAT'S THE RULE? The constant differences method of discovering a function to describe a linear sequence can be used with students in grades 5 and up. If students are not familiar with multiplication of negative integers, some teachers may be reluctant to use the activity. However, experience with many students indicates that teachers can quickly and simply teach multiplication of negative numbers and then proceed with the decreasing sequences. See the Charged Particles and Integer Patterns activities in Chapter 4 for alternative methods for teaching multiplication of integers. To avoid negative integers with lower grade students, begin with finding only the rule for increasing sequences.

Middle school students are familiar with the multiplication tables. However, the relationships among the terms of a sequence (such as 7, 12, 17, . . .), the constant difference (5), and the multiples of the constant difference may not be so apparent. Setting this activity in a Sherlock Holmes detective story will enhance students' interest in these problems. For example, if the constant difference is n, students should understand that the given sequence is related to the multiples of n. Explain that the terms in the sequence 7, 12, 17, . . . are related to the multiples of 5; in addition, someone has done something to those multiples. As detectives, it is their job to solve the mystery, what was done? That question is answered in the What Was Done? column on the Constant Differences page. For example,

$5 \times 1 = 5$ What was done to 5 to get 7?
$5 \times 2 = 10$ What was done to 10 to get 12?

Answering the What Was Done? question solves the mystery and determines the function or rule. In this case,

$$\text{Term} = 5 \times \text{Term Number} + 2$$
$$\text{Using functional notation,} \quad f(t) = 5t + 2.$$

With middle school students, functional notation should be avoided, and they should express the function (rule) in their own words or symbols that make sense to them.

• Activity

MAKING SEQUENCES

In each of the following problems, fill in the blanks with the numbers that complete the sequence. A last term is given for each sequence so that you can check your work.

1. 2, 5, 8, 11,   ____, ____, ____, ____, ____,   29

2. 8, 13, 18, 23,   ____, ____, ____, ____, ____,   53

3. 53, 46, 39, 32,   ____, ____, ____, ____, ____,   -10

4. 2, 4, 7, 11,   ____, ____, ____, ____, ____,   56

5. 4, 7, 12, 19,   ____, ____, ____, ____, ____,   103

In problems 6 through 9, follow the given rule to determine the first eight terms of each sequence.

Example: Term number times 4 plus 1

First Term	Second Term	Third Term	Fourth Term
1 x 4 + 1	2 x 4 + 1	3 x 4 + 1	4 x 4 + 1
5	9	13	17

6. Term number times 6 minus 2.

1	2	3	4	5	6	7	8	9
___	10	___	___	___	___	___	___	52

7. Term number times (-3) plus 47.

1	2	3	4	5	6	7	8	9
___	___	38	___	___	___	___	___	20

8. Term number cubed plus 5.

1	2	3	4	5	6	7	8	9
___	___	___	___	___	___	___	___	734

9. Term number squared times the next term number.

1	2	3	4	5	6	7	8	9
___	___	___	___	___	___	___	___	810

• **Activity**

CONSTANT DIFFERENCES

1. Fill in each blank below to discover a method for determining the function that describes a linear sequence of numbers.

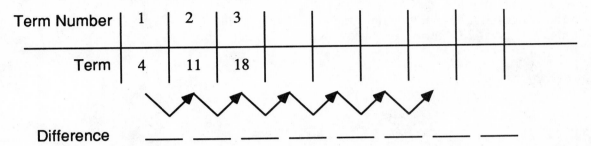

Term Number	1	2	3						
Term	4	11	18						

Difference ___ ___ ___ ___ ___ ___ ___

a. What is the constant difference? _____

Term Number	Constant Difference		What Was Done?		To Get	
1	x 7	→	7 _____	=	4	First Term
2	x 7	→	___ _____	=	11	Second Term
3	x __	→	___ _____	=	___	Third Term
10	x __	→	___ _____	=	___	Tenth Term
50	x __	→	___ _____	=	___	Fiftieth Term

b. What is the rule that generates the terms in the sequence? _____

2. Fill in each blank below, as in problem 1.

Term Number	1	2	3						
Term	26	21	16	11					

Difference ___ ___ ___ ___ ___ ___ ___

Term Number	Constant Difference		What Was Done?		To Get	
1	x -5	→	-5 _____	=	___	First Term
2	x -5	→	___ _____	=	___	Second Term
3	x __	→	___ _____	=	___	Third Term
10	x __	→	___ _____	=	___	Tenth Term

3. What is the rule that generates the terms in the sequence? _____

• Activity

WHAT'S THE RULE?

For each of the given sequences, do the following:

A. Fill in the missing numbers.
B. Determine the linear function that generates the terms in the sequence.
C. Determine the 97th and 423rd term of the sequence.

	Function (Rule)	**97th Term**	**423rd Term**
1. 9, 13, 17, 21, ____, ____, ____, ____, . . .	_____	_____	_____
2. -2, -1, 0, 1, ____, ____, ____, ____, . . .	_____	_____	_____
3. 17, 27, 37, 47, ____, ____, ____, ____, . . .	_____	_____	_____
4. 98, 96, 94, 92, ____, ____, ____, ____, . . .	_____	_____	_____
5. 3, 8, 13, 18, ____, ____, ____, ____, . . .	_____	_____	_____
6. 568, 565, 562, 559, ____, ____, ____, ____, . . .	_____	_____	_____
7. 1, 7, 13, 19, ____, ____, ____, ____, . . .	_____	_____	_____
8. 205, 197, 189, 181, ____, ____, ____, ____, . . .	_____	_____	_____
9. 18, 25, 32, 39, ____, ____, ____, ____, . . .	_____	_____	_____
10. 680, 671, 662, 653, ____, ____, ____, ____, . . .	_____	_____	_____
11. 2, 9, 16, 23, ____, ____, ____, ____, . . .	_____	_____	_____

II. LOGICAL REASONING

PURPOSE

This activity is designed to introduce students to the elimination problem solving strategy and the indirect method of reasoning.

TIME REQUIREMENT

- Elimination and Indirect Reasoning: 50 to 60 minutes
- Logical Reasoning: 20 to 30 minutes

GETTING STARTED

The Elimination and Indirect Reasoning pages should be completed first and discussed with students. Have them write some notes explaining their solutions as they complete the problems. Remind them to record the order in which they used the given clues in their reasoning.

KEY IDEAS

ELIMINATION and INDIRECT REASONING Class discussion should focus on the reasoning processes used. Each problem in the Elimination activity includes a set of clues that students must analyze individually to eliminate possible solutions. As a result of past instruction, students may approach problem solving with an algorithmic procedure, such as read the problem, start at the beginning, and work through the problem step by step. When using elimination, it may be more important to analyze all the clues and make a good choice of which one to use first.

The "which clue first" concept should be the focus of the discussion in the two number problems on the Elimination page. In problem 2, the first clue in the list may not be the easiest to use. Clues C and E are very simple first choices, followed by B and D. In problem 3, a list of possible solutions must be generated, so it becomes even more important to use a clue or combination of clues that will first determine a manageable set of possibilities.

The problems in the Indirect Reasoning activity introduce and develop the indirect method of reasoning and the use of a table to organize the data and to assist in the implementation of the strategy. Discussion of problem 1 should focus on the reasoning process used by the students. The answers to questions a and c are "no." In each case, a "yes" answer would lead to a contradiction of the known fact that "all jars are labeled incorrectly."

In these two activities, the first two problems lead the student through the process and provide either the set of possible solutions (Elimination), the organizing questions that lead to the solution, or a table that aids in the solution (Indirect Reasoning). However, problem 3 in each activity requires the student to generate the possible solutions (Elimination) or construct a table that will aid in the solution (Indirect Reasoning).

LOGICAL REASONING These four problems combine the lessons of the first two activities. In problem 1, the choice of the first clue is important. Generating a list of numbers two more than the multiples of 8 results in a shorter list than numbers that are one more than the multiples of 7. Problem 2 necessitates elimination on the basis of several criteria. Since more than one solution is possible, one must analyze the combinations of coins to determine which one yields the greatest amount.

In problem 4, the critical clue is D. If the correct answer for question 2 is "true," then the other questions have three possible combinations of answers. Since Josh claims he can determine the correct answers, the answer to question 2 must be "false."

Through discussion of these ideas, students will develop a better understanding of the process of indirect reasoning.

EXTENSIONS

These activities provide an introduction to the use of the elimination strategy. Students need many experiences to further refine the process and become confident with it. Many commercial materials are available that contain a variety of problems like those presented in this activity. Number puzzles can help to reinforce many number theory concepts. Logic problems provide additional opportunities for students to develop the indirect reasoning process. Computer software is available that allows students to develop logical reasoning processes in a variety of interesting and challenging problems.

IN THE CLASSROOM

This activity can be used with students in grades 5 through 8. In the middle grades, students should not be taught formal logic, as they are just entering the "formal operational stage" as defined by Piaget. Activities such as these provide an excellent introduction to the use of logic in these grades. Learning the process of elimination and the use of indirect reasoning in these grades provides a base for the study of more abstract reasoning in later courses.

• Activity

ELIMINATION

1. Inspector Bob E. Sleuth of the London Police Force is investigating a £1 million robbery at the Two Dot Diamond Exchange. Five suspects are in custody.

    • "Green-faced" Larry. He gets so car sick, police had to walk him to the station.

    • "Gun Shy" Gordon. He has been afraid of guns since he shot off his big toe as a boy.

    • "Loud Mouth" Louise. She is so shy, she only leaves her Aunt Jane's house at night to rent "Wild World of Wrestling" videos at the corner store.

    • "Tombstone" Teri. She works the graveyard shift running a forklift at a warehouse.

    • "Lefty" McCoy. He lost his left arm in a demolition derby accident.

    Use these clues to help Sleuth solve the crime.
    A. The sales clerk told police the robber had a large handgun.
    B. A waiting taxi whisked the robber away.
    C. The robber wore a large trenchcoat and a ski mask.
    D. The robber clowned around in front of the security cameras.
    E. The manager said the robber nervously twiddled his or her thumbs while the clerk stuffed diamonds in some sacks.

    Who should be booked and held over for trial? _____

2. Circle the number at the right that is described by the following clues.

A. The sum of the digits is 14.	2660	2570	905
B. The number is a multiple of 5.	1580	1058	1922
C. The number is in the thousands.	1355	1455	770
D. The number is not odd.	2290	2435	1770
E. The number is less than 2411	1832	860	1680

3. Solve the following number riddle.
    A. I am a positive integer.
    B. All my digits are odd.
    C. I am equal to the sum of the cubes of my digits.
    D. I am less than 300.
    Who am I? _____

• Activity

INDIRECT REASONING

1. Andrea was visiting her Uncle Roland, who had a large jellybean collection. When she asked if she could have some, he said yes, if she could solve a problem for him. He told her that he had three jars, each covered so that no one could see the color of the jellybeans. One jar was labeled *red*, the second, *green,* and the third, *red-green*. However, he said that no jar had the correct label on it. She could reach into one jar, take one jellybean, and then she had to tell him the correct color of the jellybeans in each jar. She reached into the jar labeled *red-green* and pulled out a red jellybean.

   a. Are there any green jellybeans in that jar?_____ Why?

   b. What is the correct label for the jar labeled *red-green*? _____

   c. Can the jar labeled *red* contain red and green jellybeans? _____ Why?

   d. What are the correct labels for each of the jars? _____

2. Students in the fifth grade were playing a trivia game involving states, state birds, and state flowers. They knew that in Alaska, Alabama, Oklahoma, and Minnesota, the flowers were the camellia, forget-me-not, pink-and-white lady's slipper, and mistletoe, and the birds were the common loon, yellowhammer, willow ptarmigan, and scissortailed flycatcher. No one knew which bird or flower matched which state. They called the library and received the following clues. Use the clues to complete the table below.

   A. The flycatcher loves to nest in the mistletoe.

   B. The forget-me-not is from the northernmost state.

   C. Loons and lady's slippers go together, but Minnesota and mistletoe do not.

   D. The yellowhammer is from a southeastern state.

   E. The willow ptarmigan is not from the camellia state.

State				
Flower				
Bird				

3. Each year, the Calaveras County Frog Jumping Contest is held at Angel's Camp, California. In last year's contest, four large bullfrogs, Flying Freddie, Sailing Susie, Jumping Joe, and Leaping Liz, captured the first four places. Each frog was decorated with a brightly colored bow before the competition began. From the following clues, determine which frog won each place and the color of its bow.

   A. Joe placed next to the frog with the purple bow.

   B. The frog with the yellow bow won, and the frog with the purple bow was second.

   C. The colors on Freddie's bow and Susie's bow mix to form orange.

   D. The color of the fourth bow was green.

   On a separate sheet of paper, construct a table similar to the one in problem 2 to help you organize your work.

• **Activity**

LOGICAL REASONING

In the following problems, construct a set of possible solutions based on certain clues, and then eliminate according to the other clues, or construct a table to help organize your work as illustrated on the previous pages.

1. Mike said to Linda, "Bet you can't guess the number of candies I have in this sack." "Give me a clue," she said.

   "I have more than 50 but less than 125. If you divide them into piles of 8, there are 2 left over. If you divide them into piles of 7, there is 1 left over," said Mike.

   "Oh, that's easy, you have _____ candies!!" said Linda.

   What is Linda's answer, and how did she get the answer so easily?

2. Juan claims that he knows a certain combination of U.S coins such that he cannot make change for a dollar, half dollar, quarter, dime, or nickel. Is this possible? If so, what is the *greatest* amount of money Juan could have, and what coins would they be? He does not have any silver dollars.

   Total amount = _____   Coins = _____

3. Four married couples are celebrating Thanksgiving together. The wives' names are Jolene, Jane, Marie, and Chris. Their husbands are Bob, Rick, Lee, and Lyle.

   Examine the following clues and determine who is married to whom.

   A. Rick is Jolene's brother.

   B. Marie has two brothers, but her husband is an only child.

   C. Lyle is married to Chris.

   D. Jolene and Lee were once engaged but broke up when Lee met his present wife.

4. A social studies quiz consists of five true-false questions numbered 1 through 5.
   A. There are more true than false answers.
   B. Questions 1 and 5 have opposite answers.
   C. No three consecutive answers are the same.
   D. Josh knows the correct answer to the second question.
   E. From these clues, Josh can determine the correct answer to each question.

   What are the correct answers to each of the five questions on the quiz?

SETS AND LOGIC

ACTIVITIES:
I. ATTRIBUTES
II. LOOPS

I. ATTRIBUTES

PURPOSE These activities introduce the concept of an attribute and involve sorting and classifying using a set of attribute logic pieces. The activities review and apply the elimination problem-solving strategy. Students will search for patterns, reason inductively, and make, test, and justify conjectures.

MATERIALS For each group of two or three students:

• scissors
• a copy of the Attribute Pieces page (page 21)

TIME REQUIREMENT 50 to 60 minutes

GETTING STARTED Prior to class, cut out one set of attribute pieces, and place the pieces in a paper bag. It is also a good idea to make a transparency of the Attribute Pieces page and cut out the pieces for display on the overhead. Students should complete the Attributes activities and discuss the results before doing What's Different?

ATTRIBUTES At the beginning of class, show the bag filled with attribute pieces to the students. Remove one piece from the bag, and show it to them. Ask the students what it is. After they have named the shape and described the shading, remove another piece, and ask what it is. Once the students have described the figure, ask if they can guess what else might be in the bag. If they respond with a description of one of the pieces in the bag, remove it and show it to them; otherwise, show them a different piece. Repeat this procedure until all the pieces have been identified.

WHAT'S DIFFERENT? Illustrate the idea of a one-difference train by placing one attribute piece on an overhead projector and asking students to name pieces that differ from it by *exactly one* attribute. Discuss the students' responses; then select one of the correctly identified pieces, and place it to the right of the piece on the overhead. Repeat this procedure until a one-difference train four or five pieces long has been constructed.

KEY IDEAS **ATTRIBUTES** Problem 2 involves the concept of similarity. Students should recognize that the figure they constructed had the same shape but was larger than the one on the page. This illustrates the distinction between congruent and similar figures, a distinction that can be further illustrated by comparing various pieces in the set. *When discussing congruence and similarity, it is important to turn the pieces over so that the type of shading does not confuse the concepts.*

Problem 3 focuses on the concept of symmetry. Students should recognize that, if the figure is folded along a vertical line, the two halves of the figure will coincide with each other. This means the figure has a vertical line of symmetry. Have students display the figures they created and identify what symmetries, if any, the figure possesses. *Again, when discussing symmetry, the type of shading must be ignored.*

Problem 7 illustrates a fundamental counting principle. The problem can be answered by first choosing any attribute and then multiplying the number of piles by the number of pieces in each pile, as in problem 6. However, a more efficient method is to find the product of the number of values for each of the attributes. Since there are two values for size, three values for shape, and four values for type of shading, the number of pieces in the set is 2 x 3 x 4 = 24.

The application of the counting principle can be extended by determining the number of pieces in sets with different attributes or different values. For example, suppose that the set of attribute pieces included pieces that had one hole punched in them in addition to the pieces that do not have holes. How many attribute pieces would this set contain? (Answer: 48)

ATTRIBUTE ELIMINATION Problems 8 through 11 focus on the key features of applying the elimination problem-solving strategy. When clues are given, it is a good idea to review all of them before deciding which one should be used first. A statement is usually selected first because it is the easiest to use or because it eliminates the most possibilities.

Arranging the pieces in some organized fashion also facilitates the use of the elimination strategy since it makes it possible to identify the pieces with a given attribute quickly. For example, the pieces might be organized in the following pattern:

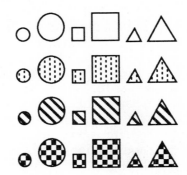

The most efficient procedure for problem 9 is to begin with the third clue. This clue eliminates all but the third row of pieces and reduces the number of possibilities to six, as opposed to eight possibilities if the first clue is used and 12 if the second is used. The first clue should be used next. This clue eliminates all but the two striped triangles and narrows the solution to two possibilities. Have students suggest the most efficient sequence in which to use the clues in problems 8, 10, and 11.

Problems 12 through 14 involve identifying common attributes. Students may answer problems 12 and 13 by saying that the plain figure does not belong since the other figures all have some type of shading. This answer is correct, but the students have missed the idea that plain is a type of shading.

WHAT'S DIFFERENT? Students should be asked to explain the process they used for constructing their difference trains.

In problem 6, regardless of the piece selected, 6 pieces will differ from it by one attribute, 11 pieces will differ by two attributes, and 6 pieces will differ by three attributes. Discuss various students' results to verify this conclusion.

The method of organizing used in problem 5 provides a clue for how to verify the conclusion in problem 6 without checking every piece. For example, sorting the two-difference pile into three groups–those that differ in size and shape, those that differ in size and shading, and those that differ in shape and shading–suggests the following argument:

Number of pieces that differ in:

shape and size	= 2 differing shapes x 1 differing size	= 2 pieces
shading and size	= 3 differing shadings x 1 differing size	= 3 pieces
shape and shading	= 2 differing shapes x 3 differing shadings	= 6 pieces
TOTAL	=	11 pieces

Similar arguments can be constructed for the number of pieces that differ by one attribute and by three attributes.

EXTENSIONS   Several software packages may be used effectively to extend these activities. *Gnee or Not Gnee* and *Odd One Out* extend the ideas in problems 12 through 14 of Attribute Elimination, and *Teddy's Playground* provides experience with difference trains. These programs are published by Sunburst Communications. *Gertrude's Puzzles*, published by The Learning Company, provides experience with logic puzzles like those in problems 7 through 9 of What's Different?

IN THE CLASSROOM   These activities may be adapted for use in grades K through 6. If commercial attribute sets are available for student use, the figure in problem 2, the table in problem 6, and all of the Attribute Elimination page can be modified to correspond to the attributes and values of the commercial set. Otherwise, copies of the Attribute Pieces page (page 21) can be copied on heavy paper for the students to cut out. For the primary grades, it is best to use four different colors of paper and use just the plain figures for the master. This results in a set where the attributes are color, shape, and size, which are easier for young children to describe.

In the upper grades, the activities may be used as presented, but several modifications are necessary when using them with students in grades K through 2. In the primary grades, all the instructions should be given orally, and problem 7 should be omitted. The concept of similarity should not be emphasized with primary students, so the figure in problem 2 should be drawn to the same scale as the attribute pieces being used. Enough copies of the drawing should be made and colored so that each group of students has at least one copy on which they can actually place the pieces. Finally, problem 5 should be discussed informally without the use of the terms *attribute* and *value*, and, since the clues for problems 8 through 12 are being given orally, discussion of the sequencing of the clues may not be appropriate.

What's Different? may also be adapted for use in grades K through 6. In the upper grades, the activity may be used as presented. In the primary grades, explanations and instructions should be given orally, and students should draw the pieces used in their solutions for questions 7 through 9 rather than writing the names. If commercial attribute block sets are used, appropriate changes must be made in problem 4 and in the table.

•Activity

ATTRIBUTES

Make a copy of the Attribute Pieces page, and cut out the pieces.

1. Experiment with the pieces.

2. Use five of the pieces to build the figure at the right.

3. Use some of the pieces to create a figure of your own. Make a drawing of your figure below.

4. Sort the pieces in some organized way. Describe how you sorted the pieces.

5. Size and shape are two attributes, or characteristics, of each piece. *Large* and *small* are the values of the size attribute.

    a. How many attributes does each piece have? _____

    b. What are the values of each of the attributes?

6. Complete the following table:

Sort the Pieces by	Number of Piles	Number in Each Pile
Size		
Shape		
Type of Shading		

7. How many attribute pieces are there in the set? _____
    Explain how you could answer this question without counting all the pieces.

· Looking Back

ATTRIBUTE ELIMINATION

In problems 8 through 11, use the clues to eliminate all but one piece. Write the name of the piece in the blank.

Example:

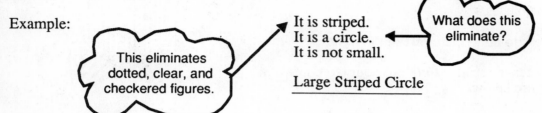

This eliminates dotted, clear, and checkered figures.

It is striped.
It is a circle.
It is not small.

What does this eliminate?

Large Striped Circle

8. It is dotted.
    It is square.
    It is not large.

    _____

9. It has three sides.
    It is not small.
    It is striped.

    _____

10. It is checkered.
    It is not a square.
    It is large.
    It is not a circle.

    _____

11. It is small.
    It is not striped.
    It is not plain.
    It is round.
    It is not dotted.

    _____

In problems 12 through 14, a set of four attribute pieces is given, but in each set one of the pieces is different from the others. For each problem, decide which piece does not belong in the given set, circle that piece, and then explain your decision.

12.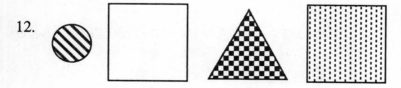

13.

14.

•Activity

WHAT'S DIFFERENT?

1. Choose one attribute piece. Choose a second piece that differs from the first piece by *exactly one* attribute. Place it to the right of the first piece. Choose a third piece that differs from the second piece by exactly one attribute. Place it to the right of the second piece. Continue this process until you have a one-difference train eight pieces long. Sketch the pieces in your train.

2. Remove the fourth piece from your train. From the set of unused pieces, name all the possible replacements for the piece you removed.

3. Construct a two-difference train by repeating the procedure in problem 1, but choose each piece so that it differs from the preceding piece by *exactly two* attributes. Sketch the pieces in your train.

4. Place all the pieces in a pile, then remove the large checkered triangle. Sort the remaining pieces into three piles as follows: place all the pieces that differ from the large checkered triangle by exactly one attribute in one pile, all the pieces that differ from the large checkered triangle by exactly two attributes in a second pile, and all the pieces that differ by exactly three attributes in the third pile. Record the number of pieces in each pile in the table in problem 6.

5. Organize the pieces in each of the piles from problem 4 in some systematic fashion. Describe what you did.

6. Repeat the procedure in problems 4 and 5 two more times. Select a different starting piece each time. Record the starting piece and the number of pieces in each pile in the table.

Original Piece	Number of Pieces Differing by		
	1 Attribute	2 Attributes	3 Attributes
Large Checkered Triangle			

What would you conclude from the data in the table?

In each of the following problems, write the name of one attribute piece in each box. Pieces in boxes connected by one line must differ by exactly one attribute, pieces in boxes connected by two lines must differ by exactly two attributes, and pieces in boxes connected by three lines must differ by exactly three attributes.

7.

8.

9.

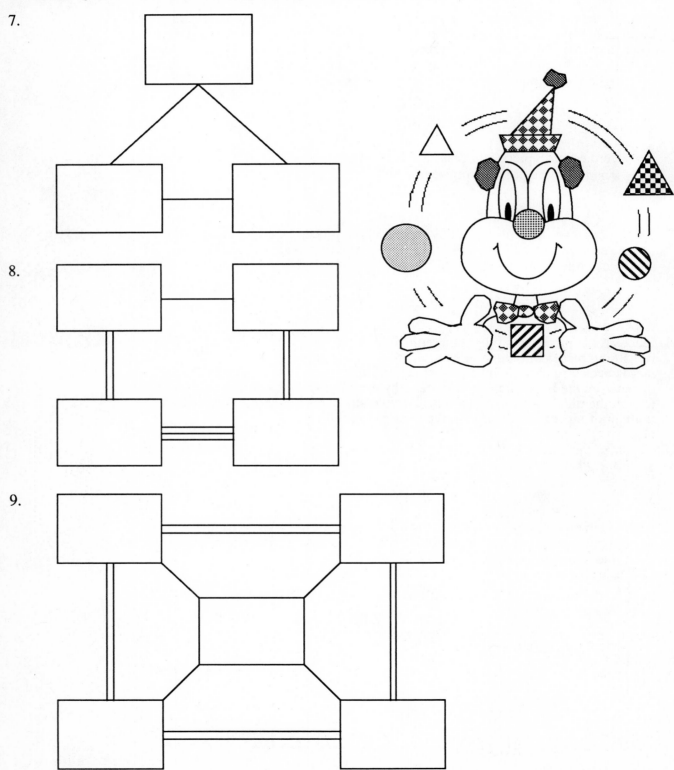

ATTRIBUTE PIECES

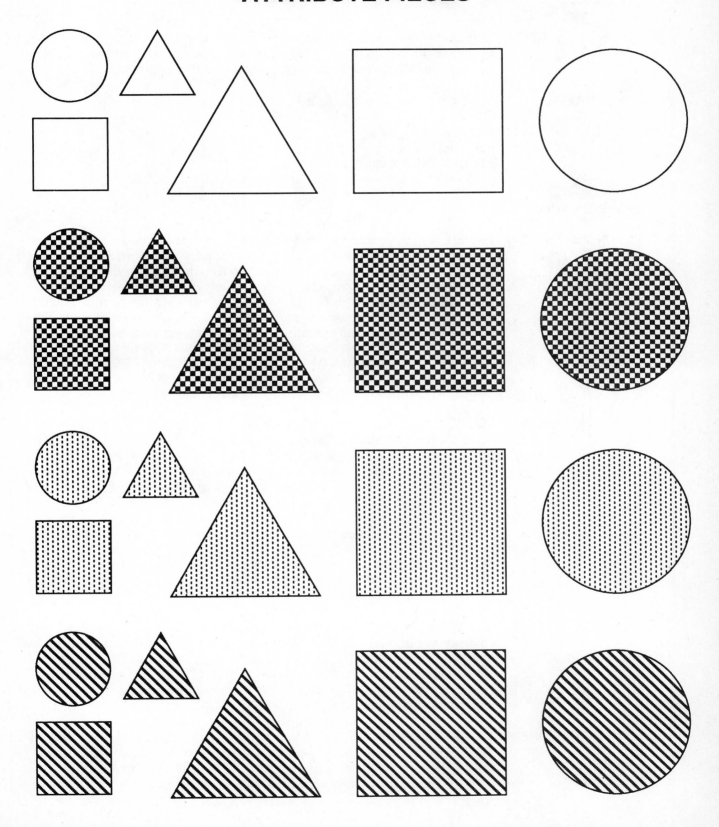

II. LOOPS

PURPOSE   This activity provides a concrete introduction to the concepts of set, subset, empty set, and inductive reasoning. Union, intersection, complement, Venn diagrams, and set notation are also introduced.

MATERIALS   For each group of two to four students:

- 1 set of attribute pieces
- 3 meters of string
- ten 3 x 5 index cards
- scissors

TIME REQUIREMENT   50 to 60 minutes

GETTING STARTED   Explain that, in problems 9 and 12 in the Loops activity, the labels may contain only one attribute value and, if necessary, the word *not*.

Before completing Loops Revisited, define the terms *set, union, intersection, relative complement,* and *universal set,* and use the results from questions 1 through 6 in Loops and a Venn diagram to illustrate the definitions. In the discussion, particular attention should be given to the relationship between the operations of union, intersection, and complement and the conjunctions *or, and,* and *not.* After this discussion, introduce the set notation for union ($\cup$), intersection ($\cap$), complement ($^{-}$), and difference (-). A similar sequence should be used to discuss problems 7 and 8 in Loops, where the concepts of empty set and subset are introduced.

KEY IDEAS   **LOOPS** The solutions to problems 9 and 12 involve indirect arguments. Have students generate a list of possible labels for the loop on the left in problem 9. The loop contains both large and small pieces, so the label does not involve the size attribute. The label could be NOT PLAIN since the loop contains pieces with all but plain shading, or the label could be NOT SQUARE since the loop contains only triangles and circles. Assume that the correct label is NOT PLAIN, and ask where the small striped square should be placed. Since it would go inside the loop, this would contradict the fact that the piece is outside the loop. Thus, the label must be NOT SQUARE. Repeat this procedure for the loop on the right, and also have students provide indirect arguments for determining the labels for the loops in problem 12.

LOOPS REVISITED This is a semi-concrete activity that develops the connection between the concrete experiences with set concepts and the use of symbolic set notation. The terminology used in the activity is not mathematically precise. For example, region C is not, technically, a set. However, the terminology used is more consistent with the level of student understanding and thus is more useful in establishing the connections.

EXTENSIONS   The loop puzzles in the computer program *Gertrude's Puzzles,* published by The Learning Company, may be used to reinforce and extend the Loops activity. Loops Revisited may be extended by using the results of problems 17c and 17h to motivate investigations of set equivalences, such as $A - B = A \cap \overline{B}$, $\overline{A \cup B} = \overline{A} \cap \overline{B}$, and $\overline{A \cap B} = \overline{A} \cup \overline{B}$.

IN THE CLASSROOM   Loops may be adapted for use in grades 3 through 8. Appropriate changes must be made in the activity if commercial sets of attribute pieces are used. Loops Revisited is most appropriate for use in grades 7 and 8.

•Activity

LOOPS

Make two loops of string approximately 1 meter in circumference. Label one loop CHECKERED and the other LARGE.

Place all the checkered attribute pieces inside the loop labeled CHECKERED and all the large pieces inside the loop labeled LARGE. Place all the other pieces outside both loops.

1.   Is it possible to place the attribute pieces as directed? _____
     Why or why not?

2.   How many pieces are inside the two loops, that is,
     how many pieces are either CHECKERED or LARGE?_____

3.   How many pieces are both CHECKERED and LARGE?_____

4.   How many pieces are CHECKERED but not LARGE?_____

5.   How many pieces are LARGE but not CHECKERED?_____

6.   Suppose the loops were labeled SQUARE and
     NOT STRIPED, as shown at the right. In which
     region, A, B, C, or D, would you place each of
     the following pieces?

     a. Large Striped Square   _____
     b. Small Checkered Triangle _____
     c. Small Plain Square   _____
     d. Large Striped Circle   _____

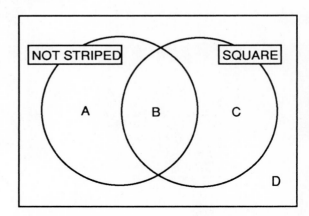

7.   What labels could be used for the loops in problem 6 so that region B would
     contain no pieces?

8.   What labels could be used for the loops in problem 6 so that region C would
     contain no pieces?

9. A few of the attribute pieces have been placed in the loops in diagram A. What are the labels for the loops? Write the answers in the boxes in the figure.

A

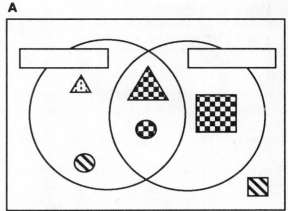

10. Make a third loop of string approximately 1 meter in circumference. Arrange and label the three loops as shown in diagram B. Place all the attribute pieces in the loops. How many pieces are in each of the following regions?

a. A _____   b. B _____   c. C _____
d. D _____   e. E _____   f. F _____
g. G _____   h. H _____

B

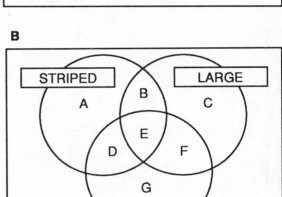

11. In which region, A through H, is each of the following pieces?

a. Large Striped Triangle   _____

b. Small Striped Circle   _____

c. Large Plain Square   _____

d. Small Checkered Triangle   _____

e. Small Dotted Circle   _____

f. Small Striped Square   _____

12. A few of the attribute pieces have been placed in the loops in diagram C. What are the labels for the loops? Write the answers in the boxes in the figure.

C

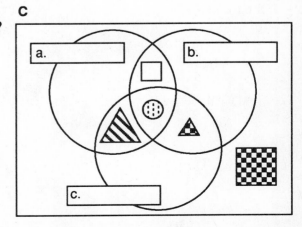

· **Looking Back**

LOOPS REVISITED

Problems 1 through 4 refer to problem 6 in the Loops activity page. For each problem, describe the attribute pieces in the given region in words and with set notation.

Example: Describe the pieces in region C.

Solution: A. Region C is the set of pieces that are square and striped.

> Alternate wording: Region C is the complement of the set of pieces that are not striped relative to the set of square pieces.

B. Region C = {square pieces} - {not striped pieces}

> Alternate solution: Region C = {square pieces}∩{striped pieces}

13. Describe the pieces in region B.

14. Describe the pieces in region A.

15. Describe the pieces that are inside the two loops.

16. Describe the pieces in region D.

17. Let the universal set, U, be the set of all attribute pieces, D = {dotted pieces}, T = {triangles}, and S = {small pieces}. First arrange and label the three loops for the sets D, S, and T, and place the attribute pieces in them. Then list the pieces in the following sets:

a. $T \cup D$ b. $S \cap D$

c. $D - T$ d. $(D \cap S) \cap T$

e. $(S \cap T) \cap \overline{D}$ f. $\overline{(D \cup S) \cup T}$

g. $T - \overline{(S \cup D)}$ h. $D \cap \overline{T}$

18. One possible answer for problem 7 in the Loops activity is to label one loop SQUARE and the other TRIANGLE.

a. What pieces are in the intersection of these sets?

b. How would you describe the intersection of the set of squares and the set of triangles?

c. Which diagram, A or B below, shows the relationship between the set of triangles and the set of squares? _____

19. One possible answer for problem 8 in the Loops activity is to label one loop CHECKERED and the other NOT STRIPED.

a. What pieces are in the intersection of these sets?

b. How would you describe the intersection of the set of checkered pieces and the set of not striped pieces?

c. How would you describe the relationship between the set of checkered pieces and the set of not striped pieces?

d. Which diagram, A or B below, shows the relationship between the set of checkered pieces and the set of not striped pieces? _____

A

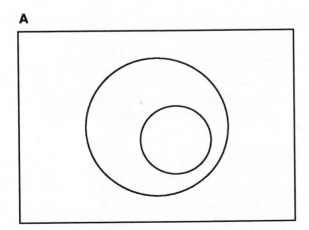

B

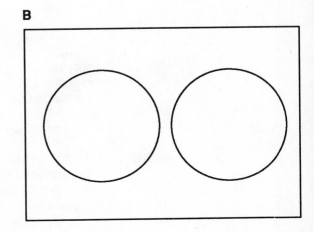

NUMERATION AND COMPUTATION

ACTIVITIES:
I. A VISIT TO FOURIA
II. LARGEST AND SMALLEST
III. TARGET NUMBER

I. A VISIT TO FOURIA

PURPOSE This activity uses a model to reinforce place value concepts, to introduce the base four system of numeration, and to develop understanding of the trading process in addition and subtraction.

MATERIALS For each group of two students:

• a pair of dice
• red, blue, and white chips, 10 of each color (counting chips, poker chips, or squares cut from tag board may be used)

TIME REQUIREMENT 50 to 60 minutes

GETTING STARTED Students should work with a partner to complete the activity.

KEY IDEAS Class discussion should emphasize the place value concepts underlying the two games. When using Fourian coins, the white, red, and blue columns on the game board represent the units ($4^0 = 1$), fours ($4^1 = 4$), and sixteens ($4^2 = 16$), respectively. That is:

$$1 \text{ blue, } 0 \text{ red, } 2 \text{ white} = 102_4 = 1 \times 4^2 + 0 \times 4^1 + 2 \times 4^0$$

Similarly, when using Tenian coins, the white, red, and blue columns represent units ($10^0 = 1$), tens ($10^1 = 10$), and hundreds ($10^2 = 100$), respectively. Since no column may contain more than three Fourian coins or nine Tenian coins, students should understand that only the digits 0, 1, 2, and 3 may be used to write base four numerals, and only the digits 0, 1, ... , 9 may be used to write base ten numerals.

EXTENSIONS The ideas regarding which digits may be used to write numerals and how the value of a digit is dependent on its position within the numeral are basic to the positional notation that underlies most systems of numeration. These ideas may be extended to other bases and to numerals containing more than three digits by using higher powers of the base. For example, for base 5,

$$1234_5 = 1 \times 5^3 + 2 \times 5^2 + 3 \times 5^1 + 4 \times 5^0$$

The coin exchanges in the games provide illustrations of the trading procedures ("carrying" and "borrowing") used in addition and subtraction algorithms. These exchanges may be extended and used to illustrate the notation used in the algorithms, as shown in the following examples:

ADDITION

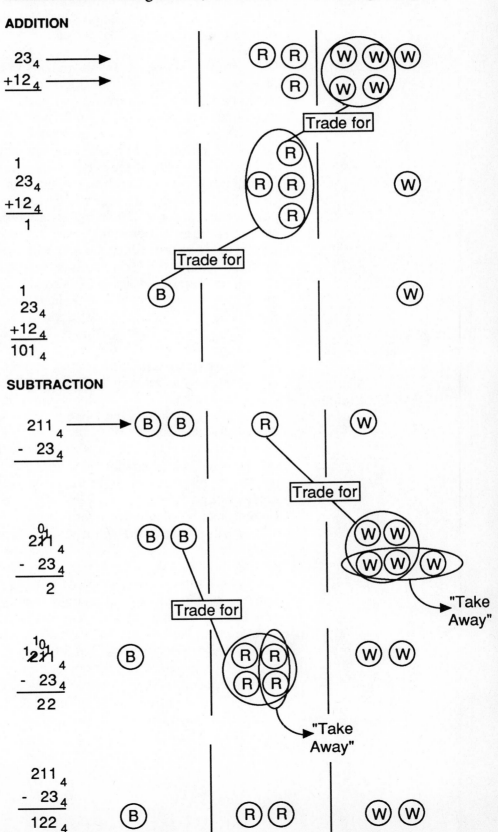

After completing the games, these examples should be explained to the students, and then students should perform several base four addition and subtraction problems on their own using the colored chip model. This procedure may also be extended by using base ten blocks to illustrate the standard algorithms for base ten addition and subtraction.

IN THE CLASSROOM

This activity may be used with students in grades 2 through 4 to reinforce place value concepts and to develop understanding of the trading procedures used in addition and subtraction algorithms. It may also be used to introduce students to other number bases. It is most effective when used as a teacher-led class activity rather than as an individual student assignment.

A Visit to Fouria combines activities that are on three different instructional levels. If the coin trading games are played without recording the result of each move, the chips and game sheet provide a *concrete* model for base four and base ten numbers and for the related place value concepts. The purpose of having students record the result of each move is to introduce the abstract concept of using a numeral to represent a number. Since the numeral for a number is derived directly from the concrete representation of the number, playing the games and recording the results is a *semi-concrete* activity. When students work with just a symbolic representation of the numbers, as in problems 4, 5, 6, and 8, they are working on the *abstract* level.

The coin trading games also provide a *concrete* model for the trading procedures used in the addition and subtraction algorithms. When the activity is extended to introduce the symbolic notation employed in the algorithm, as illustrated in the Extensions section above, it becomes a *semi-concrete* activity. When students represent borrowing and trading symbolically, without simultaneously relating them to a physical model, these activities become *abstract* .

Since the colors do not physically show the relationship between the values of the chips, the chip trading model is more abstract than most models for place value. Place value should be introduced in the primary grades using models, such as Unifix™ Cubes or bundles of sticks, that students can physically form into groups. The two coin trading games played with such materials illustrate one type of activity that may be used to introduce the concept of place value. The mathematical symbolism for writing numerals should not be introduced until students are thoroughly familiar with the regrouping process using a variety of materials.

In the next stage, students should work with materials, such as multi-base blocks, that are already grouped but that still show the relationship between the pieces. Finally, students should move on to more abstract place value models, such as colored chips, that do not show the relationship between the pieces. When the operations are introduced, the same sequence of instruction should be followed. A Visit to Fouria falls into the latter part of this instructional continuum. Thus, it is important to make sure that the students have completed the other stages before they use this activity.

•Activity

A VISIT TO FOURIA

While on an Intergalactic Numismatics Tour you encounter a meteor shower and are forced to make an unscheduled stop on the planet Fouria. The monetary system used on Fouria consists of three coins, a white coin (worth $1 in our money), a red coin, and a blue coin. The red coin is equivalent in value to four white coins, and the blue coin is equal to four red coins.

1. Unlike its sister planet, Ufouria, Fouria turns out to be a rather dull place to visit. To help pass the time, you and a fellow passenger play the coin trading game. The rules of the game are:

    A. Players alternate turns.
    B. On each turn, a player rolls one die and places that number of white Fourian coins in the White column on a Coin Trading Game Sheet.
    C. Whenever possible, a player must trade four white coins for one red coin and/or four red coins for one blue coin.
    D. Coins must always be placed in the appropriately labeled column, and no more than three of any of the coins may be in any column at the end of a turn.
    E. The first player to get two blue coins is the winner.

    Make a Coin Trading Game Sheet, and play the game with a partner. At the end of each turn, record the number of each color coin on your game sheet in a table like the one at the right.

Coin Trading Game Sheet		
Blue	Red	White

2. A third passenger has been watching you play. She suggests that it is more challenging to start the game with three blue coins and to remove white coins equal to the number rolled on each turn. The first player to remove all the coins from the playing board is the winner. Your playing partner is confused. "How can you remove white coins when there aren't any on the board?" he asks. Explain how this can be done.

Turn	Number Rolled	Result		
		B	R	W
1				
2				
3				
4				
5				
6				
7				
8				
9				
10				
11				
12				

3. Play this new version of the game with a partner. Again, record the result of each of your moves in a table such as the one above.

4. You become bored with the games and go to the spaceport newsstand to buy something to read. Glancing at the cover of a Fourian magazine, you notice that the price is given as 312_4. At the checkout stand, the clerk explains that this means three blue coins, one red coin, and two white coins. How many of each color coin does each of the following prices represent?

a. 231_4 _____

b. 102_4 _____

c. 13_4 _____

d. 20_4 _____

5. How would Fourians write each of the following prices?

a. 1 blue, 2 red, 1 white _____

b. 2 blue, 3 white _____

c. 2 white _____

d. 2 red, 3 white _____

6. Back in the waiting room, you begin leafing through a magazine that you purchased. You note that the first page is numbered 1_4, but when you get to the fourth page, you are surprised to find that it is numbered 10_4. Fill in the blanks below to show how the remaining pages of the magazine would be numbered.

1_4 _____ _____ 10_4 _____ _____ _____ _____ _____ _____

_____ _____ _____ 33_4 _____ _____ _____ _____ _____ _____

_____ _____ _____ _____ _____ _____ _____ _____ _____ _____

_____ _____ _____ _____ _____ _____ _____ _____ _____ _____

_____ _____ _____ _____ _____ _____ _____ _____ _____ _____

_____ _____ 333_4 _____ _____ _____ _____ _____ _____ _____

7. BAD NEWS! Repairs to the Intergalactic Numismatics Tour space bus will take two days. You and your game-playing friend decide to take this opportunity to visit a neighboring planet, Tenia. Amazingly, you discover that the monetary system used on Tenia also consists of three coins, a white coin (worth $1 in our money), a red coin, and a blue coin. But, on Tenia the red coin is equivalent in value to ten white coins, and the blue coin is equal to ten red coins.

Repeat problems 1 and 3, the coin trading games, using Tenian coins. On a turn, a player should roll a pair of dice and add or remove white coins equal to the number rolled, depending on which game is being played. A player may trade ten white coins for one red coin and ten red coins for one blue coin, or vice versa, but a player may have no more than nine of any one color coin in a column at the end of a turn. Record the results in a table as before.

8. a. What numeral would Tenians write for 5 blue, 9 red, 3 white? _____
    b. How would you write it? _____

II. LARGEST AND SMALLEST

PURPOSE

This problem solving activity reinforces and applies the concept of place value, helps to develop number and operation sense, and develops a deeper understanding of the role of partial products in deriving the final answer in a multiplication problem.

MATERIALS

A calculator for each student

TIME REQUIREMENT

30 to 40 minutes

GETTING STARTED

Distribute the activity page. Emphasize that, once the activity is completed, students should be able to state a rule such that, given any set of 5, 6, 7, or 8 digits, they can make two numbers, multiply them, and obtain the *largest* or *smallest* product. Be sure to encourage students to try several ways of arranging the digits before they conclude that they have derived the largest or smallest product.

Although each problem lists the specific digits to use, it is advisable to have students state the final rule in terms of digits, ordered a, b, c, d,... , where a is the smallest digit and the last letter is the largest digit. This procedure will allow all students to check their results quickly during the class discussion.

KEY IDEAS

The discussion should focus on the partial products and why a specific arrangement of digits resulted in the largest product. Students' initial intuitive idea is that the smallest digit should be placed in the ones place in the multiplier, and the largest digit should be the leftmost digit in the multiplicand. However, after some exploration, they will discover that this idea is incorrect. Given five or seven digits, students will see a pattern to the arrangements of the digits, such as :

     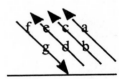

They may conclude that this pattern works with any given set of digits. However, they quickly find that, with six digits, the correct arrangement is that shown at the right. Although the pattern for a, b, and c is not the same as with an odd number of digits, the pattern of the three highest-value digits is the same.

e d a
f c b
———

In the last example above, showing the multiplication of two three-digit numbers, if d > c, then fd > fc. Therefore, the partial product fd would contribute more to the final answer than fc or ed. It is this analysis that should be discussed so that students understand why d and c should not be interchanged. The focus here is on the place value of the digits and their impact on the partial products that produce the final answer.

EXTENSIONS

As a first guess, many students may simply reverse the placement of the digits in each number to obtain the *smallest* product. For example: dca x eb becomes bce x ad. If a further guess is bde x ac, the check will verify that the assumption is false. Class discussion should focus on the placement of the three smallest digits in the two numbers and how it relates to the placement of the three largest digits when trying to obtain the *largest* product. Problems 5 through 7 apply the conclusions of the previous problems and further reinforce place value concepts and number sense.

This activity may be adapted for use when studying division. Have students chose any five digits and arrange them into two- and three-digit numbers. Divide the larger number by the smaller to obtain the largest or smallest quotient. This problem may seem trivial when using whole numbers, but it can help reinforce number and operation sense, and it develops a deeper understanding of division.

Another meaningful extension involves using decimal numbers and allowing 0 as one digit. Give students a specific set of digits, and permit various placements of the decimal point in the divisor and/or dividend. Ask students to derive either the largest or smallest quotient. Class discussion should again focus on the place value concepts and how the placement of the decimal point affects the answer. When students are deriving the largest quotient and are allowed to choose any digits, some may not consider 0 as a reasonable choice. If a two-digit divisor is being used, class discussion will quickly lead to the fact that 0.01 is the best divisor for deriving the largest quotient.

IN THE CLASSROOM

This activity can be adapted for use in grades 4 through 8. The choice of the number of digits to be used should be consistent with the students' mathematical maturity. Students at all levels should use a calculator to explore the activity and the suggested extensions. Using a calculator enables students to explore a greater variety of arrangements of digits, thus reinforcing understanding of place value as well as developing number and operation sense. It also provides a quick means for investigating the partial products so that students can verify their conjectures concerning the arrangements of the digits and can determine a rule for the arrangement that yields the largest or smallest product.

As stated in the Key Ideas section, class discussion with students should focus on the arrangements of the highest and lowest order digits in determining the largest and smallest product. Unless the partial products that involve these digits are analyzed, many elementary students will miss this important concept and thereby miss the point of the activity.

• Activity

LARGEST AND SMALLEST

1. Place the digits 1, 2, 3, and 4 in the blanks to make two two-digit numbers. Each digit may be used only once. Use a calculator to multiply the numbers. On a separate sheet of paper, try several additional arrangements of the digits to determine the arrangement that results in the largest possible product.

$$x \; \underline{\quad}\,\underline{\quad}$$
$$\overline{\underline{\qquad\qquad}}$$

2. Write the partial products for the multiplication problems you made up in problem 1. Compare the partial products that resulted in the largest product with the others. Determine a rule so that, given any four digits, you can make two two-digit numbers, multiply them, and obtain the largest possible product.

   Example :   21   4 x 1 = 4   30 x 1 = 30
                x 34   4 x 20 = 80   30 x 20 = 600

3. Place the digits 1, 2, 3, 4, and 5 in the blanks to make a two-digit and a three-digit number. Each digit may be used only once. Use a calculator to multiply the numbers. Try several other arrangements. Determine which arrangement results in the largest product.

$$\underline{\quad}\,\underline{\quad}\,\underline{\quad}$$
$$x \; \underline{\quad}\,\underline{\quad}$$
$$\overline{\underline{\qquad\qquad}}$$

4. Write the partial products for the numbers that resulted in the largest product and the partial products for one other problem. Analyze the results, and determine a rule so that, given any five digits, you can make a two-digit and three-digit number, multiply them, and obtain the largest possible product.

5. Given any seven digits, how can you place the digits into a three-digit and four-digit number, multiply the two numbers, and guarantee that you will obtain the largest possible product?

6. Does your rule also work for making two three-digit numbers from six digits?_____

7. a. Given five digits, how would you place them in a two-digit and three-digit number to obtain the smallest possible product?

   b. Given six digits, how would you place them in two three-digit numbers to obtain the smallest product?

   c. Given seven digits, how would you place them in a three-digit and four-digit number to obtain the smallest product?

III. TARGET NUMBER

PURPOSE

This activity reinforces the inverse relationship between multiplication and division, develops estimation skills, and applies the guess and check problem solving strategy.

MATERIALS

One calculator for each pair of students.

REQUIRED BACKGROUND

Students should:

• understand multiplication and division of whole numbers
• know the meaning of absolute value
• know how to use the constant operator feature on a calculator

TIME REQUIREMENT

30 to 40 minutes

GETTING STARTED

If students are not familiar with the constant operator feature, it should be explained before they start the games. Instruct each student to prepare several tables similar to the one on the activity page, and then divide the class into groups of two. Before playing each game, explain the rules and play a demonstration game with a member of the class. Emphasize that only whole numbers may be used and that the calculator may be used only to obtain the product or quotient as described in the rules for each game. All computations involved in formulating guesses must be done mentally. Before playing Games 3 and 4, specify the acceptable range for a winning result. Initially, this range may be fairly large. As students become more proficient at estimating, the range should be narrowed.

KEY IDEAS

After playing the games, students should discuss the procedures they used to formulate their guesses. In Game 1, the division tests for 2, 3, and 5 may be used to obtain two factors whose product is the target number or to help select a more challenging target. Students should also realize that they can always come within 5 of the target by using 10 as one of the factors.

Game 2 becomes trivial if students use the inverse relationship between multiplication and division. If a player chooses n and n times the target number, the quotient of these two numbers will always be the target number. Games 3 and 4 involve using rounding and the relationship between operations to estimate products and quotients as well as refining guesses based on previous results.

EXTENSIONS

The activity may be extended by allowing the use of decimals as targets, factors, quotients, or guesses. If students have access to calculators that will perform the operations with common fractions, these games may also be extended by allowing the use of fractions.

IN THE CLASSROOM

When restricted to whole numbers, these activities are appropriate for use in grades 4 through 6 to reinforce the operations of multiplication and division and to develop estimation skills. If decimals and fractions are used, the activities are appropriate for grades 4 through 8.

•Activity
_____

TARGET NUMBER

These are games for two players. Each pair will need one calculator.

GAME 1 A. The players choose a target number, and each player records it in a table like the one below. Then the players alternate turns.
B. On each turn, each player chooses two numbers (other than 1 and the target), multiplies them, and records the numbers and the product in the table.
C. If the product equals the target number, the player wins. If not, the player records the absolute value of the difference between the product and the target number in the table.
D. If neither player has won after three turns, the person with the smallest total for the three differences is the winner.

TARGET = _____			
Turn	Factors	Product	Difference
1	x		
2	x		
3	x		
		TOTAL	

GAME 2 The rules are the same as those for Game 1, except that, on each turn, each player chooses two numbers and *divides* one of them by the other to obtain a quotient. If the quotient equals the target number, the player wins. If not, the absolute value of the difference between the quotient and the target number is recorded in the table.

GAME 3 A. Player 1 chooses a target number, and player 2 chooses a constant factor.
B. On each turn, each player chooses a number and multiplies it by the constant factor to obtain a product.
C. If the absolute value of the difference between the product and the target number is less than the range specified by the teacher, the player wins.
D. If the absolute value is greater than the range, the players alternate turns until one player obtains a product within the specified range of the target number.

SAMPLE GAME

Target = 572   Factor = 17   Range = ±10

Player 1	17 x 30 = 510	Too small.
Player 2	17 x 35 = 595	Too big.
Player 1	17 x 33 = 561	Too small.
Player 2	17 x 34 = 578	Player 2 wins!

GAME 4 The rules are the same as those for Game 3, except that player 2 chooses a *constant dividend*. On each turn, each player chooses a number and divides the constant dividend by it. If the quotient is within the specified range of the target number, the player wins.

INTEGERS

ACTIVITIES:
I. CHARGED PARTICLES
II. INTEGER PATTERNS

I. CHARGED PARTICLES

PURPOSE These activities provide a concrete model for the integers and a manipulative model for introducing absolute value and the operations with integers.

MATERIALS Two different colored chips (or squares cut from tag board), 15 of each color, for each student.

REQUIRED BACKGROUND The students should be familiar with the concept of an integer.

TIME REQUIREMENT
• Charged Particles: 20 to 30 minutes
• Addition and Subtraction: 30 to 40 minutes
• Multiplication and Division: 20 to 30 minutes

GETTING STARTED Introduce the activities with a class discussion of the properties of protons and electrons.

Although it is possible to draw pictures for the models used in the activities, encourage students to use two different colored chips to represent protons and electrons and to actually manipulate the chips when completing the activities.

KEY IDEAS **CHARGED PARTICLES** A given integer can be represented in a variety of ways using the model, but the simplest representation is a set that contains only protons or electrons. In the case of zero, the simplest representation is the empty set.

In this activity, the concept of the absolute value of an integer is illustrated by the number of objects in the set for its simplest representation. This idea may be extended to the more mathematical definition that the absolute value of n is n if $n \geq 0$ or the opposite of n if $n < 0$.

ADDITION AND SUBTRACTION In this activity, students develop the rules for addition and subtraction of integers. Discussion of the activity should focus on these rules.

MULTIPLICATION AND DIVISION Discussion of this activity should focus on the interpretations of the operations and on the rules that students develop for multiplication and division of integers.

Students should realize that if the first factor in a product is positive, the "add in" interpretation of multiplication and the repeated addition interpretation are equivalent. They should also recognize that, since multiplication is commutative, problems 1c and 2a are equivalent. Since the answers to the two problems are the same, the first obtained by applying the "add in" interpretation and the second by applying the "take away" interpretation, the "take away" and "add in" interpretations are consistent with one another for products in which one factor is positive and the other is negative.

EXTENSIONS

The charged-particle model may be used to extend the operations to cases with more than two operands and to develop the associative, commutative, and distributive properties. Students should also be encouraged to find a rule for determining the sign of the product, based on whether the number of negative factors is odd or even, and to extend the rule to the odd and even powers of a negative number.

IN THE CLASSROOM

These activities provide a concrete model for the integers and a hands-on approach for introducing absolute value and the operations with integers for students in grades 5 through 8. They are most effective when used as a teacher-led class activity. Students should be familiar with the application of integers for representing temperatures, elevations, bank balances, and game scores before doing the activities.

•Activity

CHARGED PARTICLES

In the following activities, ● represents a proton, and ○ represents an electron. Protons and electrons are subatomic particles. Protons have a positive electrical charge of one unit, and electrons have a negative electrical charge of one unit. Because they have opposite charges, when a proton and an electron are paired together, they neutralize each other; that is, the pair has an electrical charge of zero.

Sets containing protons and electrons can be used to model the integers. For example:

The set at the right represents the number +2.

If the protons and electrons are paired, 2 protons are left over. The net electrical charge is +2.

The set at the right represents the number -3.

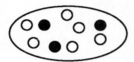

If the protons and electrons are paired, 3 electrons are left over. The net electrical charge is -3.

1.   Use two different colored chips to represent protons and electrons, and construct three more different sets that represent the number +2. Sketch them below.

2.   Use the chips to construct three different sets that represent the number -3. Sketch them below.

3.   Use the chips to construct two different sets that represent each of the following integers, and sketch them in the space provided.

   a. +5   b. -1

   c. -2   d. 0

4. Represent each of the integers in problem 3 using the least number of protons or electrons possible. Sketch your answers below.

    a.   b.

    c.   d.

5. How many total particles are in each set in problem 4?

    a. _____   b. _____   c. _____   d. _____

The answers to problem 5 are the absolute values of the integers in problem 3. The *absolute value* of an integer is the least number of protons or electrons that can be used to model it.

6. What is the absolute value of each of the following integers?

    a. -15 _____   b. +12 _____   c. 0   _____

7. What is the absolute value of

    a. +2 _____ -2 _____

    b. -3 _____ +3 _____

    c. -4 _____ +4 _____

The pairs of integers in problem 7 are called *opposites*. The opposite of an integer is its negative. An integer and its opposite have the same absolute value.

8. What is the opposite of

    a. -9 _____

    b. +7 _____

9. What integer is its own opposite? _____

•Activity

ADDITION AND SUBTRACTION

The following examples illustrate the operation of integer addition using the charged-particle model.

ADDITION

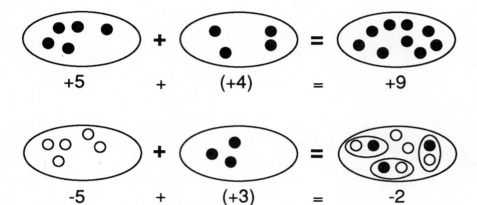

Use two different colored chips to represent protons and electrons, and manipulate them to compute the following sums. Make a drawing to illustrate what you did in each problem.

1.   +4 + (+3)   2.   +3 + (-7)

3.   -3 + (-6)   4.   +6 + (-4)

5.   -5 + (-2)   6.   -8 + (+5)

Use the charged-particle model and colored chips to investigate the following questions.

7. Is the sum of two negative numbers positive or negative? _____

8. How can you compute the sum of two negative numbers without using the model?

9. When is the sum of a positive and a negative number:

    a. equal to 0?

    b. positive?

    c. negative?

10. How can you compute the sum of a positive and a negative number without using the model?

11. Use the charged-particle model to illustrate the sum -3 + 0 = -3 in three different ways.

    a.

    b.

    c.

The following examples illustrate the operation of integer subtraction using the charged-particle model.

SUBTRACTION

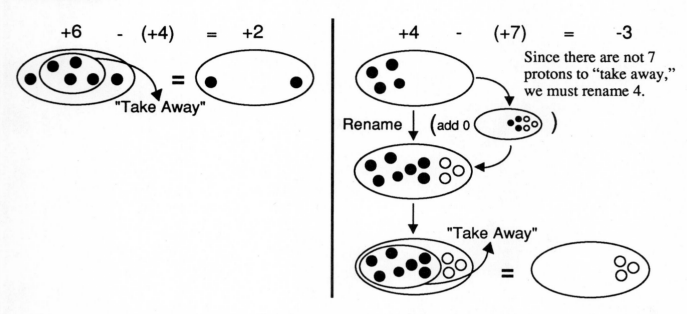

12. How could you "rename" -2 to compute the difference -2 - (+5) using the charged-particle model?

Use the charged-particle model and colored chips to compute the following differences. Make a drawing to illustrate what you did in each problem.

13. +5 - (+9)   14. +3 - (-4)

15. -2 - (+5)   16. -6 - (-5)

17. -5 - (+3)   18. -4 - (-8)

Use your answers to problems 8 and 10 to compute the following:

19. +5 + (-9) _____   20. +3 + (+4) _____   21. -2 + (-5) _____

22. -6 + (+5) _____   23. -5 + (-3) _____   24. -4 + (+8) _____

25. How do the answers to problems 19 through 24 compare with the answers to problems 13 through 18, respectively?

26. How are problems 19 through 24 related to problems 13 through 18, respectively?

27. Use the answers to problems 25 and 26 to state a rule for subtracting positive and negative numbers.

•Activity

MULTIPLICATION AND DIVISION

For positive numbers, multiplication represents repeated addition. For example, 3 x 4 = 12 means 4 + 4 + 4 = 12. However, this interpretation of multiplication will not work for products like -3 x (+4). To calculate products like this, we must alter our concept of multiplication.

In the product $n \times p$, n tells the number of times we must "add in" (if n is positive) or "take away" (if n is negative) charged particles, and p tells the type and number of particles (protons, if p is positive, and electrons, if p is negative).

Example 1:

In the product +2 x (+3), +2 means "add in" two times, and +3 means three protons. Thus +2 x (+3) means "add in" three protons two times.

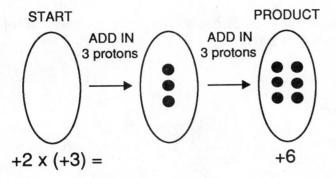

1. Use the "add in" interpretation of multiplication and colored chips to compute the following products.

   a. +3 x (+4) _____

   b. +3 x (-2) _____

   c. +4 x (-3) _____

Example 2:

In the product -2 x (+3), -2 means "take away" two times, and +3 means three protons. Thus -2 x (+3) means "take away" three protons two times.

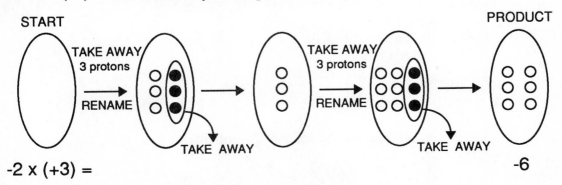

2. Use the "take away" interpretation of multiplication and colored chips to compute the following products.

    a. -3 x (+4) _____   b. -3 x (-2) _____   c. -4 x (-3) _____

3. Use the "add in / take away" interpretation of multiplication, the charged-particle model for integers, and colored chips to investigate the following questions:

    a. If both factors in a multiplication problem are positive, is the product positive or negative? _____ Explain why, using chips.

    b. If both factors in a multiplication problem are negative, is the product positive or negative? _____ Explain why, using chips.

    c. How do you compute the product?

    d. If one of the factors in a multiplication problem is positive, and the other factor is negative, is the product positive or negative? _____
        Explain why, using chips.

    e. How do you compute the product?

4. Use the answers to problem 3 to write a rule for multiplying two integers.

Multiplication and division are *inverse operations*. For example,

> $12 \div 4 = 3$ since $3 \times 4 = 12$
>   More generally, $A \div B = C$ means that $B \times C = A$.

This property can be used to help discover a rule for division of integers.

> $-12 \div (+4) = n$ Think: $(+4) \times n = -12$, so $n = -3$.
>   Thus $-12 \div (+4) = -3$.
>
> $-8 \div (-2) = n$ Think: $(-2) \times n = -8$, so $n = +4$.
>   Thus $-8 \div (-2) = +4$.

5. Use the inverse operations concept to compute the following quotients:

    a. +18 ÷ (-6) _____   b. -15 ÷ (+3) _____   c. -24 ÷ (-6) _____

6. Use the results of these examples to help you write a rule for division of positive and negative numbers.

II. INTEGER PATTERNS

PURPOSE   These activities use the patterns problem solving strategy to develop the algorithms for the operations with integers. They can also be used to reinforce the development of the algorithms for those students who have used the Charged Particles activities.

REQUIRED BACKGROUND   Students should know the concept of absolute value.

TIME REQUIREMENT   20 to 30 minutes

GETTING STARTED   Emphasize to students that the "rules" being asked for should be stated in their own language. No formal mathematical terminology should be required at this point.

In the subtraction activity, students should make all the numerical entries in problems 1 through 4 before doing problem 5, which asks for the related addition problem. Also point out to students that, when they are completing multiplication problems 1 and 3, they should stop when the product is zero and complete parts a through c before continuing to enter the remaining numerical answers.

KEY IDEAS   Class discussion should focus on the idea of analyzing pattterns as a means of mathematical discovery and learning. In these activities, each problem set is structured so that there are two distinct patterns, one in the numbers involved in the operations, the second in the answers. Attention should focus on these patterns and their relationships. The problems lead students to the discovery of the algorithms through the exploration of the patterns in the answers.

Problem 5 in the multiplication activity is a Looking Back problem. Students have previously learned that multiplication and division are inverse operations. This concept is now used to derive the rules for division of integers; no new set of problems or definitions is needed.

EXTENSIONS   Using patterns to develop or reinforce an algorithm can also contribute to the understanding of the concept of negative exponents and why a number raised to the zero power is 1. Patterns such as the following can be displayed, and class discussion can lead students to develop an understanding of these concepts.

$$10^3 = 1000 \qquad\qquad 5^3 = 125$$
$$10^2 = 100 \qquad\qquad 5^2 = 25$$
$$10^1 = 10 \qquad\qquad 5^1 = 5$$
$$10^0 = 1 \qquad\qquad 5^0 = 1$$
$$10^{-1} = \frac{1}{10} \qquad\qquad 5^{-1} = \frac{1}{5} = \frac{1}{5^1}$$
$$10^{-2} = \frac{1}{100} = \frac{1}{10^2} \qquad\qquad 5^{-2} = \frac{1}{25} = \frac{1}{5^2}$$

Class discussion should focus on such questions as:

- What is the pattern of the exponents?
- What is the pattern in the answers?
- As the exponents decrease by 1, what happens to the answers?

These questions will lead students to better understand that any number other than zero raised to the zero power is always the result of dividing the number before it in the pattern (n to the first power) by n. Thus, $n^0 = n \div n = 1$. Similarly, n^{-1} will always be $1 \div n$ or $1/n^1$, and so on for other negative exponents.

IN THE CLASSROOM   This activity is appropriate for use with students in grades 6 through 8 when the operations on integers are being introduced or reinforced. The Charged Particles activities gave students an opportunity to develop the algorithms with integers using a manipulative approach. Other contexts, such as temperature above and below zero, elevation change above and below sea level, walking backward and forward, deposit and withdrawal from a bank account, and number lines, can provide problem situations that allow students to investigate real-world applications of integers and their operations.

This activity further reinforces the development work done in these other contexts and allows students to analyze several patterns, all of which lead to the development of an algorithm. It also illustrates the consistency of mathematics. Students' analysis of patterns in the operations on whole numbers leads them to develop the algorithms for the integer operations. Some students may not be satisfied with analyzing just one pattern in order to derive a rule. They should be encouraged to develop other patterns of their own, using different numbers to illustrate the same idea.

• Activity

INTEGER PATTERNS: ADDITION

Fill in the missing entries and observe the patterns in each column of numbers. Use the completed list to answer the following questions.

1. When is the sum of a positive number and a negative number:

   a. positive?

   b. zero?

   c. negative?

2. Write a rule for adding a positive number and a negative number.

3. Write a problem situation for elementary students that illustrates the addition of positive and negative numbers.

4	+	4	=	8
4	+	3	=	7
4	+	2	=	6
4	+	1	=	5
4	+	0	=	___
4	+	-1	=	___
4	+	-2	=	___
4	+	___	=	___
___	+	___	=	___
___	+	___	=	___
___	+	___	=	___

4. Observe the pattern in the set of problems at the right, and write a rule for the addition of two negative numbers.

5. Write a problem situation for elementary students to illustrate the addition of two negative numbers.

-4	+	2	=	-2
-4	+	1	=	-3
-4	+	___	=	___
-4	+	___	=	___
___	+	___	=	___
___	+	___	=	___
___	+	___	=	___

• Activity

INTEGER PATTERNS: SUBTRACTION

In each of the following sets of problems, observe the patterns of the numbers and fill in the missing entries.

1. $4 - 0 = 4$ _____
    $4 - 1 = 3$ _____
    $4 - 2 = \underline{\ \ }$ _____
    $4 - 3 = \underline{\ \ }$ _____
    $4 - \underline{\ \ } = \underline{\ \ }$ _____
    $4 - \underline{\ \ } = \underline{\ \ }$ _____
    $4 - \underline{\ \ } = \underline{\ \ }$ _____
    $\underline{\ \ } - \underline{\ \ } = \underline{\ \ }$ _____

2. $3 - 4 = -1$ _____
    $2 - 4 = -2$ _____
    $1 - 4 = \underline{\ \ }$ _____
    $0 - 4 = \underline{\ \ }$ _____
    $\underline{\ \ } - 4 = \underline{\ \ }$ _____
    $\underline{\ \ } - \underline{\ \ } = \underline{\ \ }$ _____
    $\underline{\ \ } - \underline{\ \ } = \underline{\ \ }$ _____

3. $4 - 3 = 1$ _____
    $4 - 2 = 2$ _____
    $4 - 1 = \underline{\ \ }$ _____
    $4 - \underline{\ \ } = \underline{\ \ }$ _____
    $4 - \underline{\ \ } = \underline{\ \ }$ _____
    $4 - \underline{\ \ } = \underline{\ \ }$ _____
    $\underline{\ \ } - \underline{\ \ } = \underline{\ \ }$ _____
    $\underline{\ \ } - \underline{\ \ } = \underline{\ \ }$ _____

4. $-4 - 3 = -7$ _____
    $-4 - 2 = \underline{\ \ }$ _____
    $-4 - 1 = \underline{\ \ }$ _____
    $-4 - \underline{\ \ } = \underline{\ \ }$ _____
    $\underline{\ \ } - \underline{\ \ } = \underline{\ \ }$ _____
    $\underline{\ \ } - \underline{\ \ } = \underline{\ \ }$ _____
    $\underline{\ \ } - \underline{\ \ } = \underline{\ \ }$ _____

5. For each of the subtraction problems above, write a related addition problem using numbers with the same *absolute value* as those in the given problem.

Examples: $4 - 5 = 4 + -5$ $-4 - 1 = -4 + -1$

6. Write a rule for the subtraction of integers.

• **Activity**

INTEGER PATTERNS: MULTIPLICATION AND DIVISION

1. Fill in the missing numbers below, and observe the pattern in each column.

$4 \times 4 = 16$

   a. Describe the pattern of the second factors in the multiplication problems.

$4 \times 3 = 12$

$4 \times 2 = $ ___

   b. Describe the pattern of the products.

$4 \times$ ___ $= $ ___

$4 \times$ ___ $= $ ___   STOP : answer a-c
before continuing

   c. Since both patterns will continue, complete the table and extend the pattern to the next five multiplication problems.

$4 \times$ ___ $= $ ___

2. Write a rule for the multiplication of a positive number and a negative number.

3. Fill in the missing numbers below, and observe the pattern in each column.

$-3 \times 2 = $ ___

   a. Describe the pattern of the second factors.

$-3 \times 1 = $ ___

$-3 \times$ ___ $= $ ___   STOP : answer a-c
before continuing

   b. Describe the pattern of the products.

$-3 \times$ ___ $= $ ___

$-3 \times$ ___ $= $ ___

   c. Since both patterns continue, complete the table and extend the pattern to the next four problems.

4. Write a rule for the multiplication of two negative numbers.

5. We know that division is the inverse operation of multiplication, that is:

$A \times B = C$ implies that $A = C \div B$, and $B = C \div A$.

We can use this property to discover the rule for division of integers.

a. $-3 \times 4 = -12$ means $-12 \div 4 = $ _____ , and $-12 \div -3 = $ _____.

b. Use the results of these problems to help write a rule for division of positive and negative numbers.

NUMBER THEORY

ACTIVITIES:
I. THE SQUARE EXPERIMENT
II. INTERESTING NUMBERS
III. POOL FACTORS

I. THE SQUARE EXPERIMENT

PURPOSE
This activity develops the concepts of prime, composite, and square numbers through the geometric model of rectangular arrays. Students will also discover the complete factorization of a number. The activity is most effective for developing these concepts, and it may also be used to reinforce these ideas with students who have not used the activity.

MATERIALS
For each student, 30 small square tiles or squares cut from tag board (graph paper may be used instead of squares).

REQUIRED BACKGROUND
Students should know how to construct a rectangular array.

TIME REQUIREMENT
30 to 45 minutes

GETTING STARTED
Be sure that students understand the directions regarding the construction of a rectangular array. In geometry, two polygons are congruent if all their corresponding sides and angles are congruent. This is true regardless of the orientation in the plane or in space. However, for the purposes of this activity, students must understand that there is a difference between ☐☐ and ⊟ and that these will be considered as two distinct arrays.

It is helpful to have the students work in pairs to build the necessary arrays. This pairing encourages students to work together and reduces the time needed to build all the arrays as students can share results.

KEY IDEAS
This activity develops the connection among the definitions of several mathematical terms and a geometric model that illustrates the essence of the definitions. For example, prime numbers are those numbers that have exactly two factors. In the activity, a prime number of chips determines exactly two arrays. By constructing all the rectangular arrays determined by a given number of chips, students physically model the complete factorization of a number.

The connection between square numbers and their related geometric model is a significant element of this activity. Not only is a square number associated with the geometric figure of a square, but a square number is also unique, in that it determines an odd number of arrays and thus has an odd number of factors. This unique feature should be explored by asking such questions as:

• Why are there an odd number of arrays?
• How is this different from the rectangular arrays of other composite numbers?

Students may talk about the fact that a 1 x 3 array may be rotated to a 3 x 1 array, but a 5 x 5 array rotates and is still 5 x 5. This discovery leads students to realize that factors are always paired, and, because of this fact, most of the numbers in the Total Number of Arrays column of Table 1 are even.

Another important aspect of the activity is that it illustrates the uniqueness of the number 1. Many people have the false impression that 1 is a prime number since it fits the general understanding of the definition of *prime*. The placement of 1 alone in Column A in Table 2 clearly indicates that it is in a category by itself and does not belong to the set of prime numbers. Once again, the connection between the number concept and the geometric model helps to emphasize this distinction and reinforce the definition of *prime numbers*.

EXTENSIONS

This activity provides a setting in which students can explore pairs of factors of a given number and begin to understand the rationale behind the division algorithm used in computer programs for finding all the factors of a number. Having completed the activity, students can write the complete factorization of numbers, such as :

16	1 x 16	36	1 x 36	24	1 x 24
	2 x 8		2 x 18		2 x 12
	4 x 4		3 x 12		3 x 8
			4 x 9		4 x 6
			6 x 6		

If the factors are arranged in order as shown, students discover that the factors always occur in pairs. Thus, when division results in a zero remainder, *two* factors are determined, the quotient and the divisor. By investigating factors for square numbers, they also discover that, once division by all integers from 1 to the square root of the number is completed, all the factors have been determined. This discovery leads to greater efficiency in an algorithm for finding all the factors of a given number. Rather than dividing by every number from 1 to the number, first find its square root. If the root is an integer, the square root is a factor. Now divide the number by all integers from 1 to the greatest integer less than the square root. Whenever the remainder is zero, a pair of factors is determined.

IN THE CLASSROOM

This activity is appropriate for students in grades 5 through 7. The vertical and horizontal orientation of a figure may need some explanation so that the desired relationships among the number of arrays, the complete factorization, the number of factors, and the geometric model are clear.

When first introducing the number theory concepts described, it may be useful to have students explore arrays for numbers through 30. Simply extend Table 1, and change the numbers in problems 2 and 3 to some other composite number, such as 48, and some other square number, such as 49, respectively. Students using this activity as an introduction to these concepts will not know the correct mathematical names for problem 6. Rather than answering students' questions, these names should be brought out in general class discussion, and their definitions should be related to the connections between the number theory concepts and the geometric model.

If students have been introduced to these number theory concepts but have not completed the activity, it can be used to reinforce the concepts by demonstrating the connections between the number theory concepts and the geometric model. In this situation, students progress rapidly through the completion of Table 1, and class time may be spent discussing the concepts and reinforcing the definitions of terms as related to the model. The activity can then be extended by completing the Looking Back problems and exploring the ideas in the Extensions section.

• Activity

THE SQUARE EXPERIMENT

Use squares or graph paper to form all the rectangular arrays possible with each different number of squares. Record your results in Table 1.

| Number of Chips | 1 | 2 | 3 |

Arrays

Note : □ is not a rectangular array.

When describing an array by its dimensions, the figure ⊏⊐ has a base of 2 units and an altitude of 1 unit and is therefore labeled 2 x 1. The figure is labeled 1 x 2.

TABLE 1

Number of Squares	Dimensions of the Rectangular Arrays	Total Number of Arrays
1		
2		
3	1 x 3, 3 x 1	2
4		
5		
6	1 x 6, 6 x 1, 3 x 2, 2 x 3	4
7		
8		
9		
10		
11		
12		
13		
14		

1. Use the results from Table 1 to complete Table 2.

TABLE 2

List the Numbers of Squares That Produced:			
A	**B**	**C**	**D**
Only One Array	Only Two Arrays	More Than Two Arrays	An Odd Number of Arrays

2. Suppose that you had 24 chips.

   a. How many rectangular arrays could be made?_____

   b. In which column(s) in Table 2 would you place 24?_____

   c. What are the factors of 24? _____

3. a. What are the factors of 16?_____

   b. How many rectangular arrays can you make with 16 chips?_____

   c. In which column(s) of Table 2 would you place 16? _____

4. Look at the data in Table 1. How is the number of factors of a given number related to the number of rectangular arrays?

5. a. Why is it that the numbers in column D of Table 2 produce an odd number of arrays?

   b. What are the next three numbers that would be placed in column D?

   _____

6. What is the mathematical name for the numbers in

   a. column B? _____

   b. column C? _____

   c. column D? _____

7. Which numbers can be placed in two lists?   _____
   Why?

8. Can any numbers be placed in three lists?   _____
   If so, which ones?

• Looking Back

For the following problems, sets A, B, C, and D are the sets of numbers in columns A, B, C, and D, respectively, of Table 2. Find each of the following.

9. $C \cap D$ _____

10. $\overline{A}$ _____

11. $B \cap C$ _____

12. $\overline{B} \cap \overline{C}$ _____

13. $\overline{B \cup C}$ _____

14. $C \cup D$ _____

II. INTERESTING NUMBERS

PURPOSE
This activity applies the concepts of prime number, perfect cube, perfect square, odd number, even number, and prime factorization. Patterns are used to discover a rule for determining the number of factors of a given number from its prime factorization.

MATERIALS
A calculator for each student.

REQUIRED BACKGROUND
Students should:

• know how to determine the prime factorization of a number
• know the definition of a palindrome

TIME REQUIREMENT
70 to 80 minutes

GETTING STARTED
Students should work in groups of three or four and use calculators when completing these activities. Also, if a computer program that generates the factors of a number is available, students should be encouraged to use it to generate data and check results when doing the activity.

KEY IDEAS
INTERESTING NUMBERS Students should discover that, to find a number with a high interest rating using the Interest Rating Scale, it is advantageous to look for numbers with many factors.

NUMBER OF FACTORS Discuss the students' results, and provide additional practice applying the rule that has been discovered. Then provide an informal proof of the conjecture using the fundamental counting principle.

Example: The prime factorization of 360 is 2^3 x 3^2 x 5^1. So, if n is a factor of 360, then n must have the form 2^x x 3^y x 5^z, where $x = 0, 1, 2,$ or 3, $y = 0, 1,$ or 2, and $z = 0$ or 1. Since there are four possibilities for the value of x, three possibilities for y, and two for z, there are 4 x 3 x $2 = 24$ ways to choose the three exponents and, therefore, 24 factors of 360. This argument can be generalized to any positive integer greater than 1.

EXTENSIONS
This activity may be extended with such questions as:

• What is the smallest perfect cube that has 72 as a factor?
• What is the largest perfect square that is a factor of 2940?
• If n is the pth power of a positive integer, what can you conclude about the exponents in the prime factorization of n?

IN THE CLASSROOM
Middle school students normally learn prime factorization, but usually they only see it applied in determining greatest common factors and least common multiples for use in renaming fractions. Consequently, they rarely develop an appreciation for the fundamental role of prime factorization in mathematics. This activity is appropriate for students in grades 6 through 8. It may be used as presented here to demonstrate an application of prime factorization and inductive reasoning.

·Activity

INTERESTING NUMBERS

The lyrics of an old song assert that "One is the loneliest number." This makes 1 interesting, but all numbers have some property that makes them interesting.

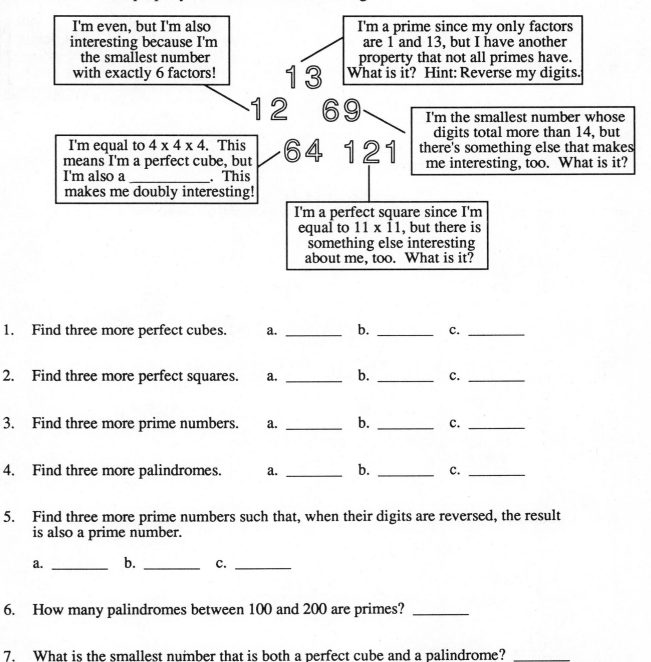

I'm even, but I'm also interesting because I'm the smallest number with exactly 6 factors!

I'm a prime since my only factors are 1 and 13, but I have another property that not all primes have. What is it? Hint: Reverse my digits.

I'm equal to 4 x 4 x 4. This means I'm a perfect cube, but I'm also a _____. This makes me doubly interesting!

I'm the smallest number whose digits total more than 14, but there's something else that makes me interesting, too. What is it?

I'm a perfect square since I'm equal to 11 x 11, but there is something else interesting about me, too. What is it?

13 12 69 64 121

1. Find three more perfect cubes.   a. _____   b. _____   c. _____

2. Find three more perfect squares.   a. _____   b. _____   c. _____

3. Find three more prime numbers.   a. _____   b. _____   c. _____

4. Find three more palindromes.   a. _____   b. _____   c. _____

5. Find three more prime numbers such that, when their digits are reversed, the result is also a prime number.

    a. _____   b. _____   c. _____

6. How many palindromes between 100 and 200 are primes? _____

7. What is the smallest number that is both a perfect cube and a palindrome? _____

Now let's use the rating scale at the right to investigate some interesting three-digit numbers.

Example: 169

Perfect Square (169 = 13 x 13)	7 points
Sum of Digits Greater Than 14 (1 + 6 + 9 = 16)	4 points
Odd Number	2 points
Three Factors (1, 13, and 169)	3 points
Interest Rating	16 points

INTEREST RATING

Prime Number	15 points
Perfect Cube	10 points
Perfect Square	7 points
Sum of Digits Greater Than 14	4 points
Even Number	3 points
Odd Number	2 points
Each Factor	1 point

8.   Choose any three-digit number. Find its interest rating using the scale.

 a. Number _____   b. Interest Rating _____

9.   Can you find a three-digit number with an interest rating greater than 30 points? _____
 Explain.

10. What is the greatest interest rating you can get for a prime number? _____
 Explain.

11. a. Explain why a number that is greater than 1 and both a perfect cube and a perfect square would have an interest rating of at least 24 points.

 b. Are there any three-digit numbers that are both perfect cubes and perfect squares?

 c. If so, what are their interest ratings?

12. Try to find the three-digit number with the highest interest rating.

• **Looking Back**

NUMBER OF FACTORS

To have a high interest rating, a number must have a large number of factors. In this activity, you will discover a way to determine how many factors a number has without calculating all the factors.

13. The following table classifies numbers by the number of factors they have. Fill in the six answer blanks in the table.

14. Choose four more two-digit composite numbers. Determine the prime factorization and the number of factors of each number. Add these data to the table.

Numbers With							
1 Factor		**2 Factors**		**3 Factors**		**4 Factors**	
Number		Number	Prime Factorization	Number	Prime Factorization	Number	Prime Factorization
1		2 3 5	2^1 3^1 _____	4	2^2	6	$2^1 \times 3^1$
5 Factors		**6 Factors**		**7 Factors**		**8 Factors**	
Number	Prime Factorization	Number	Prime Factorization	Number	Prime Factorization	Number	Prime Factorization
		12	$2^2 \times 3^1$			24	_____
9 Factors		**10 Factors**		**11 Factors**		**12 Factors**	
Number	Prime Factorization	Number	Prime Factorization	Number	Prime Factorization	Number	Prime Factorization
____	$2^2 \times 5^2$	____	$2^4 \times 5^1$			60 72	_____ _____

15. Look at the prime factorizations for 2, 3, 4, 5, 8, and 9. Each of these numbers has only one prime factor. How is the total number of factors of each number related to the exponent in its prime factorization?

16. Use your answer from problem 15 to find a number that has

    a. 5 factors. _____

    b. 7 factors. _____

    c. 11 factors. _____

    Check your predictions by listing the factors of each number.

17. Now look at the prime factorizations of 6, 20, 24, and 36. Each of these numbers has more than one prime factor. How is the total number of factors of each number related to the exponents in its prime factorization? Hint: Don't forget the result of problem 15.

18. Does the relationship you discovered in problem 17 predict the number of factors of 60, 72, 80, and 100 correctly? Explain why or why not.

19. What is the prime factorization of 360? _____

20. Determine the number of factors of 360 by using the exponents in the prime factorization and by listing.

21. State a general rule for determining the number of factors of any given number from its prime factorization.

22. What is the smallest positive number that has exactly 100 factors?

    Hint: 12, 18, and 32 all have six factors. $12 = 2^2 \times 3^1$ and $6 = 2 \times 3$

    $$18 = 2^1 \times 3^2$$
    $$32 = 2^5$$

    Analyze other sets of numbers that have the same number of factors in a similar fashion, and look for a pattern.

III. POOL FACTORS

PURPOSE   This activity provides a geometric problem setting that applies the concepts of greatest common factor (GCF), least common multiple (LCM), and relatively prime numbers.

MATERIALS   For each student:

- graph paper
- a straightedge

REQUIRED BACKGROUND   Students should understand the concepts of GCF and LCM.

TIME REQUIREMENT   30 to 40 minutes

GETTING STARTED   The directions for the activity and the example should be reviewed so that students understand the terminology and the correct procedure for counting the number of "hits."

Instruct students to construct various models of pool tables on graph paper, label the pockets, and trace the path of the ball. Emphasize the fact that the ball must always pass through the corners of the squares. Data for each pool table should be entered in the table. If the dimensions of the table are relatively prime, students will quickly discover a rule for finding the number of squares and hits. If the only models drawn are those with relatively prime dimensions, suggest that they use other numbers. As a hint to the solution, suggest multiples of the dimensions on a table previously drawn.

KEY IDEAS   It is possible that students will discover the rules to determine the number of hits and number of squares but will state them without using the wording GCF or LCM. Since the phrase "relatively prime" may not be part of the students' vocabulary, their explanation of a rule for the number of hits may include such ideas as "when the two numbers don't have any common factors except 1, ..." In doing so, they have correctly communicated the definition of relatively prime numbers and have connected the idea to the problem situation that gave rise to the concept.

These situations should be capitalized on by the teacher since students are describing these concepts without using formal mathematical language. Class discussion will help students to better understand the definitions and to formalize their mental constructs of these concepts at a level consistent with their mathematical maturity.

What students should discover:

Number of hits = (altitude + base) ÷ (GCF of the altitude and the base)
Number of squares = LCM of the altitude and the base

EXTENSIONS   This problem can be extended by exploring a more difficult question, "Into which pocket does the ball finally fall?" To assist in solving this problem, have students add another column on the table as shown at the top of page 64.

Add this column for Extension ↓

Altitude	Base	Number of Hits	Number of Squares	Final Pocket

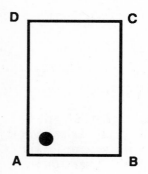

Students should be encouraged to look back at the first part of the activity to see what ideas can be applied to the solution of this question. To determine the final pocket, let:

J = Altitude ÷ (GCF of the Altitude and the Base)
K = Base ÷ (GCF of the Altitude and the Base)

If J is odd and K is even, final pocket is B.
If J is odd and K is odd, final pocket is C.
If J is even and K is odd, final pocket is D.
The ball never goes into Pocket A.

IN THE CLASSROOM   This problem solving activity can be used with students in grades 7 and 8 who have previously studied the concepts of GCF and LCM. Since the idea of relatively prime numbers may not be familiar to students, this activity also offers an excellent opportunity to introduce it and its application to GCF and LCM.

• Activity

POOL FACTORS

A. Draw several pool tables with different dimensions on graph paper. Label the pockets A, B, C, and D in order, starting with the lower left pocket as shown below.

B. Place a ball on the dot in front of pocket A.

C. Shoot the ball as indicated by the arrows so that it always travels on the diagonals of the grid and rebounds at an angle of 45 degrees when it hits a cushion. ·

D. Count the *number of squares* that the ball travels through.

E. Count the *number of hits* as the ball hits a cushion, the initial hit at the dot, and the hit as the ball goes into a pocket.

In the table below, enter the dimensions of each pool table, the number of squares the ball travels through, and the number of hits. Analyze the data in the table, and determine a rule so that you can predict the number of squares and the number of hits, given the dimensions of any pool table.

Altitude	Base	Number of Hits	Number of Squares
4	6	5	
5	7		
3	2		

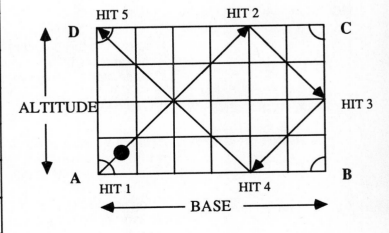

RATIONAL NUMBERS

ACTIVITIES:
I. SQUARE FRACTIONS
II. PEOPLE PROPORTIONS
III. POPULATION STUDIES

I. SQUARE FRACTIONS

PURPOSE This activity provides a means for introducing and reinforcing the concept of a fraction and illustrating the operations with fractions using a geometric model. The activity reviews the classification of triangles and quadrilaterals and similarity and congruence of triangles. It also provides a problem situation in which students need precise oral directions so that they can construct correct figures.

MATERIALS For each student:

- one sheet of paper (20 cm to 30 cm square colored construction paper works very well)
- scissors (optional)

REQUIRED BACKGROUND Students should:

- know the basic concepts of fractions
- be familiar with the operations with fractions
- understand the geometry vocabulary used in the activity

TIME REQUIREMENT 50 to 60 minutes

GETTING STARTED Although students can do this activity alone or in small groups, the best results will be obtained when it is used as a teacher-led class activity. Use the questions on the activity pages as a script, and lead the class through the activity, demonstrating each of the folding and cutting procedures. By doing so, you will have a physical example of each shape used in the activity to show to students as you ask the questions. If students do complete the activity outside class, encourage them to work in groups so that they can discuss the questions as they complete the activity.

KEY IDEAS   Students may use a third figure to determine what fractional part one figure is of another. For example, triangle 4 fits into square 5 twice and into trapezoid D three times, so the ratio of the area of square 5 to the area of trapezoid D is 2 to 3. The area of the square is 2/3 of the area of the trapezoid. Comparing one figure with the others by physically manipulating the objects provides an opportunity to develop the concept of a fraction as the ratio of two numbers. When answering the questions, students may not use the word *area*. Mathematically, it is not correct to exclude the word *area* in an answer, but this should not become an issue in this activity. A simple explanation should be made when this point first arises so that students can focus on the important aspects of the activity and not get so distracted by vocabulary that the essential concepts are missed.

Questions such as those in problems 22 through 29 should be explored as they arise in the activity. When answering question 10b, "Triangle 3 is what fractional part of triangle A?", students may respond that triangle 3 is 1/2 of triangle 1, and triangle 1 is 1/2 of triangle A, so triangle 3 is 1/4 of triangle A. This illustrates that 1/2 of 1/2 is 1/4. In so answering, students are progressing from the concrete to the semi-abstract and should then continue to the abstract idea that $1/2 \times 1/2 = 1/4$. Several examples like this should be explored so that students can experience going from concrete to abstract and from abstract to concrete. As an example of the latter, have students explain which figures could be used to demonstrate that $1/2 \times 1/3 = 1/6$ and $1/2 - 5/16 = 3/16$.

The activity contains many questions on geometry as well as fraction concepts. Both topics may be explored at the same time. However, if students are not familiar with the vocabulary and classification of geometric figures, you may wish to skip those parts at this time and use the activity again when studying geometry. Students should physically measure the sides and angles of the triangles when determining proportionality and verifying similarity or congruence.

Problem 30 should be explored at length if the activity is being used to reinforce concepts in geometry. The fundamental difference between congruence and equality will surface during the discussion. Although shapes 3, 5, and 7 are equal in one attribute, area, they have different sizes and shapes and a different number of sides. Also, the measurements of the sides and angles are not the same. The word *equal* refers to only *one* measure of the polygons, the area. However, *congruence* means that the measures of *all* the corresponding sides and angles of the polygons are equal.

EXTENSIONS   Some extensions are suggested by problems 22 through 30. Many more such problems can be explored so that students can observe a concrete model for the operations with fractions. Subtraction can be investigated by simply restating the inverse operation of problem 28. Division can also be demonstrated. For example, 1/2 ÷ 1/4 can be modeled by comparing triangles A and 1 with the original square and asking, " How many times will triangle 1 fit into triangle A?"

Geometric questions have been included. However, the activity could be adapted so that other applications such as the following could be investigated without referring to fractions:

• What two figures are congruent?
• What two figures are similar?
• What is the ratio of the sides of the similar figures?
• What is the ratio of the areas of the similar figures?

- How does the ratio of the areas compare with the ratio of the length of the corresponding sides?
- What are the similarities and differences among squares, parallelograms, and trapezoids?
- What properties of a square are not properties of a parallelogram, and vice versa?
- What properties of a parallelogram are not properties of a trapezoid, and vice versa?
- Can a trapezoid be a parallelogram? Why or why not?

IN THE CLASSROOM   This activity can be used in several grades (4 through 7) for various content areas (such as fractions and geometry) as well as for different topics within a content area (such as the concept of fractions and operations with fractions). Problems are included on the activity pages that provide examples for each of these content areas. However, the questions posed to students should be adapted so that they are consistent with the grade level and the content area being studied. When using the activity as an introduction or review of the concepts of fractions, questions on geometry can be eliminated, and if the focus is on geometry, one should develop questions that focus on the geometric concepts being studied and skip those questions that deal with fractions.

• Activity

SQUARE FRACTIONS

Follow the folding and cutting directions carefully. If scissors are not used, make a sharp crease in the paper, and tear along the crease. Answer each question as you proceed through the activity.

Fold the square along a diagonal and divide it into two pieces by cutting along the fold.

1. What is the geometric name for the polygons formed?

   _____

2. How are the two polygons related?

3. Each polygon is what fractional part of the original square? _____
   Explain.

Pick one of the triangles; fold it as shown so that two congruent polygons result. Cut along the fold, and label the polygons 1 and 2.

4. What are the geometric names for polygons 1 and 2?

   a. _____   b. _____

5. How are the two polygons related in area?
   Explain.

6. Triangle 1 is what fractional part of triangle A?

   _____

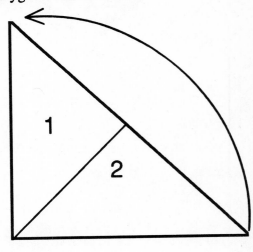

Note: In the rest of this activity, the large triangle will be referred to as triangle A.

7. Triangle 1 is what fractional part of the original square? _____
   Explain.

Locate the midpoint of the longest side of the remaining large triangle. Fold the vertex of the right angle to match the midpoint of the longest side, and crease the paper on a line as shown below. Cut along the fold to divide the triangle into two pieces, and label the polygons B and 3 as shown.

8. What are the geometric names for polygons B and 3?

    a. _____   b. _____

9. How is triangle 3 related to:

    a. triangle 1? _____

    b. triangle A? _____

10. Triangle 3 is what fractional part of:

    a. triangle 1? _____   b. triangle A? _____

    c. the original square? _____   d. trapezoid B? _____

Using the isosceles trapezoid, fold one of the endpoints of the longest side to the midpoint of that side. Crease sharply, and cut along the fold. Label the resulting polygons C and 4 as shown.

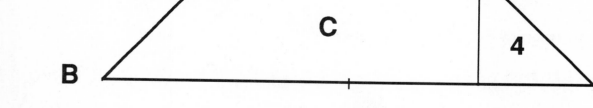

11. What are the geometric names for polygons C and 4?

    a. _____   b. _____

12. How is triangle 4 related to:

    a. triangle 3? _____

    b. triangle 1? _____

    c. triangle A? _____

13. Triangle 4 is what fractional part of:

    a. triangle 3? _____

    b. triangle 1? _____

    c. triangle A? _____

    d. trapezoid C? _____

    e. trapezoid B? _____

    f. the original square? _____

On trapezoid C, fold the vertex of the right angle at one endpoint of the shortest of the parallel sides to match the other endpoint as shown. Crease the paper, and cut along the fold. Label the resulting polygons D and 5 as shown.

14. What are the geometric names for polygons D and 5?

    a. _____

    b. _____

15. Square 5 is what fractional part of:

    a. trapezoid C? _____

    b. triangle 4? _____

    c. triangle 3? _____

    d. trapezoid B? _____

    e. trapezoid D? _____

    f. triangle 1? _____

    g. triangle A? _____

    h. the original square? _____

16. Trapezoid C is what fractional part of:

    a. trapezoid D? _____

    b. square 5? _____

    c. triangle 1? _____

    d. the original square? _____

17. For each part of problem 16, explain how you arrived at your answer.

On trapezoid D, fold the vertex of the right angle on the longest of the parallel sides to match the opposite vertex as shown below. Crease the paper on the fold. Cut and label the last two polygons 6 and 7 as shown.

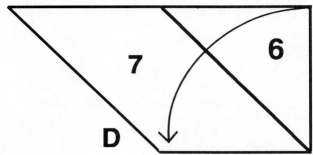

18. What are the geometric names for polygons 6 and 7?

a. _____   b. _____

19. Triangle 6 is what fractional part of:

a. trapezoid D?   _____   b. triangle A?   _____

c. trapezoid C?   _____   d. triangle 3?   _____

e. parallelogram 7?   _____   f. trapezoid B?   _____

g. square 5?   _____   h. the original square? _____

20. Trapezoid D is what fractional part of:

a. trapezoid C?   _____   b. triangle 3?   _____

c. trapezoid B?   _____   d. triangle 1?   _____

21. Parallelogram 7 is what fractional part of:

a. trapezoid D?   _____   b. triangle 1?   _____

c. triangle 4?   _____   d. triangle 3?   _____

e. square 5?   _____   f. trapezoid B?   _____

g. triangle A?   _____   h. the original square? _____

i. trapezoid C?   _____

22. Use triangle 1, triangle A, and the original square to illustrate the concept 1/2 = 2/4.

23. Use triangle 4, triangle 3, and trapezoid B to illustrate the concept 1/3 = 2/6.

24. In problem 13d, explain a method for deriving the answer that illustrates the connection between the fraction 1/5 and the ratio 1 to 5.

25. In problem 15e, explain a method for deriving the answer that illustrates the connection between the fraction 2/3 and the ratio 2 to 3.

26. In problem 7, explain a method for deriving the answer that illustrates that 1/2 of 1/2 is 1/4. Show the connection between this wording and multiplication of fractions.

27. In problem 13f, explain how one can use triangle 4, triangle 3, triangle A, and the original square to illustrate that 1/2 of 1/2 of 1/4 is 1/16. Show the connection to multiplication.

28. If the original square is one unit, use trapezoid D and square 5 to illustrate the addition problem, 3/16 + 1/8 = 5/16.

29. If trapezoid B is one unit, use triangle 4 and square 5 to illustrate the addition problem, 1/6 + 1/3 = 1/2.

30. When asked to compare shapes 3, 5, and 7, many persons will say, "They are equal." Evaluate this statement with regard to congruence and equality. The figures are all different; two are quadrilaterals, one is a triangle. The lengths of the sides are not the same, and the measures of the angles are different. How can the figures be "equal"?

II. PEOPLE PROPORTIONS

PURPOSE
This activity involves students in the process of measurement, reinforces the concept of ratio, and applies ratios in a real-world setting. It also illustrates that the comparison of ratios is easier when the ratios are expressed as decimals rather than as fractions.

MATERIALS
For each student:

- a calculator
- two 150 centimeter tapes for each group of four or five students

REQUIRED BACKGROUND
Students should:

- understand the concept of a ratio
- be able to measure lengths to 0.5 cm accuracy
- know how to change a fraction to a decimal

TIME REQUIREMENT
50 to 60 minutes

GETTING STARTED
Divide the class into groups of four or five, preferably with a mix of female and male students. For students to get a good idea of comparisons of body measurements, have them measure their hand span, the largest spread between the tip of the thumb and the tip of the middle finger. Have them wrap their hands around their wrists to compare the hand span with the circumference of the wrist; they will be about equal. Both hands can be placed around the neck; thus the neck circumference is twice the hand span or wrist circumference. For most bodies, if one places the tips of the middle fingers together at the waist, the two hand spread will be approximately one half the distance around the waist. Thus the neck is one half of the waist circumference, and the wrist is one fourth of the waist circumference. The data from Table 1 should be used to complete the fractional form in Table 2. Problems 1 and 2 should be answered before converting the fractions to decimals. The measurements will generally be diverse, and few students will recognize that the fractions for any one ratio are approximately the same, except for wing span to height, which is approximately 1 to 1.

KEY IDEAS
Students generally realize that simple ratios, such as 1/2 or 2/5, offer an easy comparison of two numbers and that 1/3 and 2/6 are equivalent. However, when students are given numbers such as those derived in this activity, it is not until the ratios are written as decimals that the comparisons become clear. Students need to learn that, even though the fractions are equivalent to the decimal values, decimals may be easier to use when making comparisons among several ratios.

Once the ratios have been converted to decimal form, students will observe how small the range of data is for any one ratio. If measurements are done carefully , the decimals may differ only in the hundredths or thousandths place. Given the decimal equivalents, students will recognize that the tibia to height ratio is approximately 1 to 4 and that the radius to height ratio is about 1 to 6. However, students will rarely recognize these ratios when reviewing only the fractions because of the diversity of the numbers in the numerators and denominators.

EXTENSIONS   This activity can motivate students to explore many fascinating examples of the application of ratios. The golden ratio abounds in nature, music, and art. The Fibonacci sequence offers another connection among the numbers in the pattern, the golden ratio, and natural phenomena. This activity can be easily extended to study how an increase in one ratio affects related ratios by analyzing some fantasy characters, such as Godzilla or the Ten Foot Chicken. Few people understand how an increase in one measurement—for instance, height—affects increases in the related measurements of area or volume. When the height of the chicken increases by a factor of 10, the mass, which is related to the volume, increases by a factor of 1000, and the cross-sectional area of the leg bone increases by 100.

Students may find these explorations exciting and interesting, and they will continue to investigate new challenges if provided with direction and resources. Some questions that might be explored are:

- Would the legs of the Ten Foot Chicken support its weight?
- Could the Ten Foot Chicken walk?
- What would happen if Godzilla jumped off a twenty story building?
- Could a giraffe have the body of a hippo?
- Why are hippos always found near water?
- Could an eagle flap its wings as fast as a humming bird, or could a humming bird soar like an eagle? Why?
- We have fossilized footprints and complete skeletons of great dinosaurs. How can we use footprints of contemporary animals to estimate the speed of these ancient animals?
- Could you outrun a dinosaur?

The navel to floor to height ratio is one of the many examples of the golden ratio on the human body. The golden ratio is the most famous of all ratios because of its application in art, music, nature, architecture, physiology and psychology, phyllotaxis, and mathematics. If the bodies measured in this activity conform to the golden ratio, then the decimal for the navel to floor to height ratio should be approximately the golden ratio, or 0.618034. Students should explore the golden ratio, investigate its occurrence in other fields, relate it to the golden rectangle, and determine the value of the ratio algebraically. A sample problem follows.

Example:

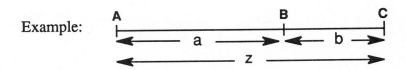

The line segment AC is divided into two segments by B. If AC = z, AB = a, and BC = b, and if z/a = a/b, then a is a golden section of z. If we let b = x and a = 1, then x+1 / 1 = 1 / x. Solve for x.
a. What is the decimal equivalent for x? _____
b. What is the reciprocal of the decimal? _____
c. What is the relationship between the value of the decimal and the value of its reciprocal?

IN THE CLASSROOM

This activity is most appropriate for grades 6 and up. These students generally have poor number sense and do not recognize that several fractions with very different numerators and denominators may represent approximately the same value. The Extensions section provides an exciting problem setting for the study of ratios for students at this age. Such explorations illustrate the connection of mathematics to many other subjects and provide meaningful problems to motivate the study of mathematics.

Some excellent resources for information about the golden ratio and other interesting questions like those given above are: *The Divine Proportion*, H.E. Huntly, Dover Publications; *Mathematics: Life Science Library*, Time-Life Books; *On Being the Right Size,* J.B.S. Haldane, Vol. 2, The World Of Mathematics; and "Restatement: How Do I See It?" from *The Challenge of the Unknown* video series, American Association for the Advancement of Science.

• Activity

PEOPLE PROPORTIONS

Paleontologists may find only a few bones of an ancient animal and yet be able to construct an entire skeleton from them. In a modern application, a forensic medical examiner may assist law enforcement agencies by providing the height, weight, age, sex, and other features of a body from its remains. In some cases, as little as a skull or two or three bones is all that is needed.

How is this possible? How can we know the appearance of a person or an animal that lived millions of years ago when we have no pictures or complete skeletons? How can an entire skeleton of an ancient animal or human be reconstructed from so little evidence?

The answer lies in the consistent ratios of the measures of various bones in bodies, regardless of the size or shape of the body.

To understand how scientists reach their conclusions, measure the body parts listed below for yourself and four other students. All measurements should be in centimeters and rounded to the nearest 0.5 cm. When making the measurements, follow the directions below:

A. Height and navel to floor: measure without shoes
B. Wing span: measure finger tip to finger tip with arms outstretched
C. Tibia: rest the foot on the floor, measure from the ankle bone to the top of the tibia on the outside of the kneecap
D. Radius: rest the elbow on the desk with the hand up, measure from the tip of the elbow to the wrist bone

Enter the name of the person and each measurement for that person in Table 1.

TABLE 1

Name of Person	Height	Navel to Floor	Wing Span	Wrist	Radius Bone	Neck	Tibia Bone

Use the measurements of the five people in Table 1, and write the fractional form for the ratios in the F columns in Table 2. Do not convert the fractions to decimals.

TABLE 2

Name of Person	Wing Span Height		Navel to Floor Height		Tibia Height		Radius Height		Wrist Neck	
	F	D	F	D	F	D	F	D	F	D

1. Examine the ratios for the five people that you measured. Are any of the ratios nearly the same for all people? _____   Which ones?

2. Is it difficult to make comparisons among the ratios in any column of Table 2? Explain.

3. Now convert all the fractions to decimals, rounded to the nearest thousandth. Compare the decimal equivalents for each of the ratios. Which ratios are approximately the same for all people? _____

4. What appears to be the ratio for wing span to height? _____ For wrist to neck? _____

5. Find the average (mean) of the decimal ratios for tibia to height and radius to height. For any given body, the tibia bone is approximately what fraction of the height (state as a simple fraction)? _____   The radius is what fraction of the height (state as a simple fraction)? _____

6. Find the average of the ratios for navel to floor to height as a decimal. _____ For height to navel to floor. _____

7. The average ratio for navel to floor to height for all humans closely approximates 0.618034. Compare this decimal with the average from your group in problem 6.

8. Write the reciprocal for the decimal 0.618034. _____   What did you find? Can you find any other decimal with this property?

9. You should have found that the ratios for all the people in your group were approximately the same. Would you expect the same results for people of any age, size, or shape? Find some other people whose age or size differs from the ones you measured, and determine if the ratios are about the same as those of your group.

III. POPULATION STUDIES

PURPOSE

This activity applies the concepts of ratio, proportion, and percent in social studies. It develops number sense, deeper understanding of the operations, and facility in the use of a calculator.

MATERIALS

A calculator for each student.

REQUIRED BACKGROUND

Students should understand ratio, proportion, and percent.

TIME REQUIREMENT

20 to 30 minutes

GETTING STARTED

This activity may be completed independently. No special instructions are required.

KEY IDEAS

Students frequently encounter numerical data, such as population densities and population growth rates, in the social sciences, but they often do not fully comprehend the information the data convey.

If Montana were as densely populated as New Jersey, over 60% of the population of the United States would be living in Montana. If New Jersey were as sparsely populated as Montana, it would have only the population of a small city. In fact, if the entire population of Japan were moved to California, California would still not be as densely populated as New Jersey. Hong Kong is 14 times as crowded as New Jersey, and the average space for each person is only about the size of a typical home in the United States. If the population of Hong Kong were spread out evenly over its area, each person would be within 14 meters of four other people. Comparisons such as these give meaning to the density figures.

When working problems 1 and 2, students should use the raw data for population and area to set up a proportion and determine the value of the missing term. If they simply multiply the area by the population density from the table, they will obtain an incorrect answer because of the rounding.

Problem 6 illustrates how a relatively small change in the population growth factor can have a significant effect over a long period of time. Students should realize that, when population increases at a constant rate, the time required to double the population is independent of the size of the initial population. Thus the problem can be simplified by starting with an initial population of 1. Students using a four-function calculator can simply count the number of times they must multiply by 1.023 before the product is greater than or equal to 2 (these multiplications can be facilitated by using the constant multiplier feature if the calculator has one). Students using calculators with an exponent key may use Guess and Check to obtain the answer.

EXTENSIONS

The activity should be extended by having students determine the population densities of their city, county, and state and comparing the results with other cities, counties, and states. Students should be encouraged to give explanations for the similarities and differences they observe.

Another interesting extension is to obtain population data from the U. S. Census Bureau for a city or state for the past 100 years and use it to explore questions like the following:

- At what rate is the population increasing?
- What would you predict the population to be in the year 2000?

- During what time periods was the rate of population growth greatest or least? Why?
- Compare population densities at ten- or twenty-year intervals. When was the population density greatest or least? Why?

To answer the questions, students may need to plot the data on a graph and explore various methods of trend analysis, such as computing moving averages. They will also need to identify patterns in population movement, such as from rural to urban or from urban to suburban, and the reasons for these changes.

IN THE CLASSROOM   This activity may be used with students in grades 5 through 8 after the concepts of ratio, proportion, and percent have been introduced. This activity is very effective when used in a geography or social studies class, where students apply these concepts to similar problems.

•Activity

POPULATION STUDIES

1.   Complete the following table. Round your answers to the nearest hundredth.

State or Nation	Population	Area (sq km)	Population Density
California	26,365,000 [a]	404,815	
Montana	826,000 [a]	376,564	
New Jersey	7,562,000 [a]	19,342	
Brazil	143,300,000 [b]	8,511,957	
Hong Kong	5,700,000 [b]	1,031	
Japan	121,500,000 [b]	371,857	
United States	241,000,000 [b]	9,171,032	

SOURCE: *The 1987 Information Please Almanac*   [a]1985 estimate   [b]1986 estimate

2.   a.   If Montana had the same population density as New Jersey, how many people
        would be living in Montana? _____

     b.   What percent of the population of the United States would be living in Montana? _____

3.   a.   If New Jersey had the same population density as Montana, how many people
        would be living in New Jersey? _____

     b.   How would you describe the population of New Jersey in this case?

4.   If all of the people in Japan moved to California, what would be the population density of
     California? _____

5.   a.   If the area of Hong Kong could be divided into congruent squares and each
        resident placed at the center of one square, how many square meters of living
        space would each person have? _____

     b.   How many meters would each person be from the nearest neighbor? _____

     c.   How does the answer in part a compare with the living space in your home?

6.   Estimate the answers to the following questions, then use a calculator to check
     your estimates.

     a.   The population of Brazil is increasing at a rate of 2.3% per year. At this rate,
        about how many years will it take for Brazil to double its population? _____

     b.   If the rate of population growth decreased by 0.5% per year, about how many
        years would it take for the population of Brazil to double? _____

     c.   If the rate of population growth increased by 1.0% per year, about how many
        years would it take for the population of Brazil to double? _____

DECIMALS AND PERCENTS

ACTIVITIES:
I. PATTERNS IN REPEATING DECIMALS
II. FLEX-IT
III. TARGET NUMBER REVISITED

I. PATTERNS IN REPEATING DECIMALS

PURPOSE This activity reviews the procedure for finding the decimal equivalent of a fraction and applies the patterns problem-solving strategy to predict the decimal equivalent of a fraction whose denominator is composed only of 9's or of a block of 9's followed by one or more 0's. The results are extended to discover rules for determining whether the decimal equivalent of a given fraction terminates or repeats and for predicting the number of digits between the decimal point and the repeating block.

MATERIALS A calculator for each student.

REQUIRED BACKGROUND Students should:

- know how to find the prime factorization of a number
- know how to convert a fraction to a decimal
- be able to obtain more digits in the decimal equivalent of a fraction than the eight or ten digits normally displayed on a calculator

TIME REQUIREMENT
- Decimal Patterns: 50 to 60 minutes
- Repeating Decimals: 50 to 60 minutes

GETTING STARTED Decimal Patterns and Repeating Decimals are independent activities. It is not essential to work the first activity before doing the second. However, the activities are most effective if Decimal Patterns is completed and discussed before students do Repeating Decimals.

Before beginning the activities, it may be necessary to explain how to obtain more digits in the decimal equivalent of a fraction than are normally displayed on a calculator.

KEY IDEAS **DECIMAL PATTERNS** This activity develops an intuitive understanding of the fact that every repeating decimal can be expressed as a fraction in which the denominator has the form

$$\underbrace{9\ldots9}_{p \text{ nines}}\underbrace{0\ldots0}_{q \text{ zeroes}}$$

where p is the number of digits in the repeating block and q is the number of digits between the decimal point and the repeating block.

Examples: $0.\overline{142857} = \dfrac{142857}{999999} = \dfrac{1}{7}$ $p = 6$ and $q = 0$

$0.12\overline{24} = \dfrac{1212}{9900} = \dfrac{101}{825}$ $p = 2$ and $q = 2$

The fact that a terminating decimal is equivalent to a repeating decimal in which the repeating block is a 9 (for example, $1 = 0.\overline{9}$ and $0.5 = 0.4\overline{9}$) is developed in problems 3c through 7.

REPEATING DECIMALS This activity develops rules for determining whether the decimal equivalent of a fraction repeats or terminates and for predicting the number of digits between the decimal point and the repeating block when the decimal equivalent does repeat. The fact that the decimal equivalent of a fraction terminates if and only if 2 and/or 5 are the only prime factors of the denominator of the fraction may be justified informally as follows:

If a fraction that is in simplest form is equivalent to a terminating decimal, then it is equivalent to a fraction in which the denominator is a power of ten.

Example: $\dfrac{1}{200} = 0.005$. Since $0.005 = \dfrac{5}{1000}$, $\dfrac{1}{200} = \dfrac{5}{1000}$

Since the denominator of the original fraction must be a factor of this power of ten (in the example, 200 is a factor of 1000), and since the only prime factors of a power of ten are 2 and 5, it follows that the only possible prime factors of the denominator of the original fraction are also 2 and 5.

Conversely, if the denominator of a fraction in lowest terms has only 2 and/or 5 as its prime factors, then the fraction can be converted to an equivalent fraction in which the denominator is a power of ten by multiplying both the numerator and denominator by either a power of 2 or a power of 5.

Examples: $\dfrac{1}{200} = \dfrac{1}{2^3 \times 5^2} = \dfrac{1}{2^3 \times 5^2} \times \dfrac{5}{5} = \dfrac{5}{2^3 \times 5^3} = \dfrac{5}{1000}$

$\dfrac{1}{250} = \dfrac{1}{2^1 \times 5^3} = \dfrac{1}{2^1 \times 5^3} \times \dfrac{2^2}{2^2} = \dfrac{4}{2^3 \times 5^3} = \dfrac{4}{1000}$

Since a fraction in which the denominator is a power of ten is equivalent to a terminating decimal, the original fraction is equivalent to a terminating decimal.

An informal justification for the result in problem 16 can be obtained by observing the fact that, if the denominator of a fraction in lowest terms is

$$2^x \times 5^y \times n$$

where n is a natural number that is relatively prime to 2 and to 5, then the fraction is equivalent to a fraction in which the denominator is

$$10^s \times n$$

where s is the greater of x and y.

Example: $\dfrac{1}{150} = \dfrac{1}{2 \times 5^2 \times 3}$ $(x = 1, y = 2, s = 2, n = 3)$

$$= \dfrac{1}{2 \times 5^2} \times \dfrac{1}{3}$$

$$= \dfrac{1}{2 \times 5^2} \times \dfrac{2}{2} \times \dfrac{1}{3}$$

$$= \dfrac{1}{10^2} \times \dfrac{2}{3}$$

$$= \dfrac{1}{100} \times 0.\overline{6}$$

$$= 0.00\overline{6}$$

In this example, multiplying by 1/100 in the final product has the effect of inserting two zeroes between the decimal point and the repeating block.

Example: $\dfrac{1}{6} = \dfrac{1}{2 \times 3}$ $(x = 1, y = 1, s = 1, n = 3)$

$$= \dfrac{1}{2} \times \dfrac{1}{3}$$

$$= \dfrac{1}{2} \times \dfrac{5}{5} \times \dfrac{1}{3}$$

$$= \dfrac{1}{10^1} \times \dfrac{5}{3}$$

$$= \dfrac{1}{10} \times 1\dfrac{2}{3}$$

$$= \dfrac{1}{10} \times 1.\overline{6}$$

$$= 0.1\overline{6}$$

In this example, multiplying by 1/10 in the final product moves the decimal point to the left of the 1, thus placing one digit between the decimal point and the repeating block.

EXTENSIONS These activities may be extended by introducing the algebraic procedure for converting a repeating decimal to a fraction. This extension should lead to exploration of the question, "Are there any decimals that are not equivalent to a fraction?" and the discovery of irrational numbers.

Problem 5 may be extended by exploring addition and subtraction of infinite decimals. For example:

$$0.12112111211112111112... + 0.21221222212222122221... = 0.\overline{3}$$

This extension may be used to show that the sum of two irrational numbers may be a rational number.

If students have access to a computer program that uses the division algorithm to display as many digits in the decimal equivalent of a fraction as desired, they may extend the activity by exploring the number of digits in the repeating block of unit fractions in which the denominator is a prime. This activity should lead to exploration of the question, "If the denominator of a fraction has the form

$$2^x \times 5^y \times p \times q$$

where p and q are primes, how is the number of digits in the repeating block related to p and q?"

IN THE CLASSROOM These activities are appropriate for students in grades 7 and 8 after they have learned how to convert a fraction to a decimal. The activity provides practice with the conversion procedure and develops a greater understanding of the division algorithm, the relationship between a fraction and its decimal equivalent, and the fundamental role of prime factorization.

The type of informal reasoning experiences in these activities provides the semi-abstract experiences necessary to aid students' transition to the more abstract reasoning required in high school mathematics. It may be necessary to modify the activity by providing more examples before asking the students to formulate conjectures. This is particularly true for problems 12 through 14 in Decimal Patterns and for the Repeating Decimals activity.

•Activity

DECIMAL PATTERNS

1. Use a calculator to convert each of the following fractions to its decimal equivalent. If your calculator rounds off answers, be careful not to be fooled by the result it displays!

    a. $\dfrac{1}{9}$ _____

    b. $\dfrac{3}{9}$ _____

    c. $\dfrac{6}{9}$ _____

    d. $\dfrac{4}{9}$ _____

    e. $\dfrac{8}{9}$ _____

    f. $\dfrac{5}{9}$ _____

2. Use the results in problem 1 to answer the following questions:

    a. How many digits appear in the repeating block of the decimal equivalent of each fraction? _____

    b. How many 9's are in the denominator of each fraction? _____

    c. What is the relationship between the numerator of each fraction and its decimal equivalent?

3. Use your answers in problem 2 to predict the decimal equivalent of each of the following fractions:

    a. $\dfrac{2}{9}$ _____

    b. $\dfrac{7}{9}$ _____

    c. $\dfrac{9}{9}$ _____

4. Convert $\dfrac{1}{3}$ and $\dfrac{2}{3}$ to decimals. What is the sum of your answers? _____

5. What does $\dfrac{1}{3} + \dfrac{2}{3}$ equal? _____

6. What do you conclude from your answers to problems 3c, 4, and 5?

7. Use the result in problem 6 to help find the fraction equivalent to each of the following decimals: (Hint: $0.0\overline{9} = 0.1 \times 0.\overline{9}$)

    a. $0.0\overline{9}$ _____

    b. $0.00\overline{9}$ _____

    c. $0.000\overline{9}$ _____

    d. $0.4\overline{9}$ _____

    e. $0.12\overline{9}$ _____

    f. $0.576\overline{9}$ _____

8. Use a calculator to convert each of the following fractions to its decimal equivalent:

   a. $\dfrac{13}{99}$ _____

   b. $\dfrac{16}{99}$ _____

   c. $\dfrac{5}{99}$ _____

   d. $\dfrac{47}{99}$ _____

   e. $\dfrac{78}{99}$ _____

   f. $\dfrac{36}{99}$ _____

9. Use the results in problem 8 to answer the following questions:

   a. How many digits appear in the repeating block of the decimal equivalent of each fraction? _____

   b. How many 9's are in the denominator of each fraction? _____

   c. What is the relationship between the numerator of each fraction and its decimal equivalent?

10. Predict the decimal that is equivalent to each of the following fractions. Then use a calculator to check your prediction.

   a. $\dfrac{213}{999}$ _____

   b. $\dfrac{783}{999}$ _____

   c. $\dfrac{2435}{9999}$ _____

   d. $\dfrac{59}{9999}$ _____

   e. $\dfrac{52063}{99999}$ _____

   f. $\dfrac{2451}{99999}$ _____

11. State a rule for finding the decimal equivalent of any *proper fraction* whose denominator is composed of 9's only.

12. Explain how the rule in problem 11 could be extended to include *improper fractions*, such as $\dfrac{23}{9}$ and $\dfrac{156}{99}$.

13. Explain how the procedure in problem 12 and the fact that $\dfrac{23}{90} = \dfrac{23}{9} \times \dfrac{1}{10}$ can be used to predict the decimal expansion of $\dfrac{23}{90}$.

14. Use the procedure in problem 13 to predict the decimal that is equivalent to each of the following fractions. Then use a calculator to check your predictions.

   a. $\dfrac{19}{90}$ _____

   b. $\dfrac{67}{90}$ _____

   c. $\dfrac{583}{900}$ _____

   d. $\dfrac{28}{990}$ _____

   e. $\dfrac{898}{900}$ _____

   f. $\dfrac{2785}{9900}$ _____

• **Looking Back**

REPEATING DECIMALS

In the course of converting fractions to their decimal equivalents, you should have observed the following:

- Some fractions convert to terminating decimals; others, to repeating decimals.
- In some fractions that convert to a repeating decimal, the digits begin repeating immediately; in others, one or more digits appear between the decimal point and the repeating block.

In this activity, you will investigate the answers to the following questions:

- Is there a way to predict whether the decimal equivalent of a given fraction terminates or repeats?
- If the decimal equivalent of a fraction repeats, how many digits will appear between the decimal point and the repeating block?

In this activity, the term fraction *refers to a fraction expressed in simplest form* .

Complete the table on page 89. Then use the data in the table to answer the following questions. If necessary, check fractions other than those in the table.

15. a. Which prime numbers appear in the prime factorization of the denominators of those fractions whose decimal equivalents terminate?

    b. Does the prime factorization of the denominator of any of the fractions whose decimal equivalents repeat contain *only* the primes found in part a? _____ If so, which fractions?

    c. How can you predict whether the decimal equivalent of a given fraction terminates or repeats?

16. a. For the fractions whose decimal equivalents terminate, how is the number of digits in the decimal equivalent of the fraction related to the exponents in the prime factorization of the denominator?

    b. Does the relationship in part a hold for the number of digits between the decimal point and the repeating block in those cases where the decimal equivalent of the fraction repeats? _____

    c. How can you predict the number of digits between the decimal point and the repeating block in the decimal equivalent of a fraction?

Fraction	Decimal Equivalent	Repeating or Terminating?	Prime Factorization of Denominator	Number of Digits in Repeating Block	Between Decimal and Repeating Block
$\frac{2}{3}$	$0.\overline{6}$	Repeats	3^1	1	0
$\frac{29}{90}$		Repeats	$2^1 \times 3^2 \times 5^1$	1	1
$\frac{17}{99}$					
$\frac{19}{3500}$					
$\frac{17}{200}$		Terminates			3
$\frac{1}{6}$					
$\frac{1}{8}$					
$\frac{7}{15}$					
$\frac{3}{125}$					
$\frac{1}{140}$					2
$\frac{3}{100}$	0.03	Terminates			
$\frac{17}{400}$					
$\frac{119}{5000}$					
$\frac{4179}{4950}$					
$\frac{1}{7}$					
$\frac{99}{260}$					
$\frac{2}{35}$					
$\frac{7}{20}$					
$\frac{5}{24}$					
$\frac{121}{600}$					

II. FLEX-IT

PURPOSE   This activity reinforces the concept of percent and applies the concept of percent increase in a personal problem setting.

MATERIALS   For each group of four or five students:

- a 100-centimeter tape
- a calculator

REQUIRED BACKGROUND   Students should know:

- how to measure to the nearest 0.5 cm
- the concept of percent
- how to determine percent increase

TIME REQUIREMENT   30 to 40 minutes

GETTING STARTED   Divide the class into groups of four or five students, preferably with a mix of female and male students in each group. Remind students to enter the names of each person in the group in the table on page 92 and then to predict the rank order of increase they expect for each person for each percent increase to be determined. This should be done *before* any measuring is done.

KEY IDEAS   The idea of percent increase or decrease is often misunderstood. Many people believe that a large percent increase is directly related to a large initial number, or, in this activity, to having large muscles. The mind set of associating a large percent increase with large initial values is difficult to dispel through practice with routine problems. This activity, however, frequently produces results exactly opposite to students' intuitive beliefs. In many cases, the largest percent increase will occur with one of the smallest female students. This result emphasizes the fact that a large percent increase depends on a large difference between the initial and final measurement relative to the initial measurement, *not* on a large initial measurement.

Because this unexpected result often occurs, the connection between the mathematical concept (percent increase) and the problem setting helps students to better understand the process of determining percent increase or decrease.

EXTENSIONS   A study of the uses of percent in advertising, discount pricing in store sales, and news stories can produce many interesting and challenging problem situations to extend this activity. For example:

1. The population of a small Third World country is increasing at a rate of 5% per year. How long will it be before the population doubles?

2. On the West Coast, some areas show an annual 16% increase in home prices. How long will it take a home to triple in price at this rate?

3. In 1945, the first electronic computer, ENIAC, was built. It could perform 5000 operations per second. In 1990, the fastest super-

computers operated at speeds greater than 100 billion operations per second. What was the percent increase over this 45-year period? What was the average annual percent increase?

4. The U.S. Census Bureau reported the following figures for the population of the country and certain geographical regions of the country in 1970 and 1980:

Region	1970	1980
United States	203.3 million	226.5 million
Northeast	49 million	49.1 million
South Atlantic	37 million	40.2 million
West	34.8 million	43.2 million

   a. What is the percent increase for the country and for each of these regions during this ten-year period?

   b. How can you account for the regional differences in increases in population?

   c. On the basis of the previous data, predict the population for 1990 and 2000.

5. A favorite candy bar advertises "15% more candy bar for the same price."

   a. What do you think the 15% increase represents: length? weight? volume?

   b. If there is a 15% increase in length, is this also a 15% increase in the weight or volume of candy?

   c. If you determine that there is a 15% increase in length without an increase   in the weight or volume, would you indeed be receiving "15% more candy at the same price"?

As a Looking Back activity to follow the Flex-It activity, have students measure the height and foot length without shoes of each person in their group. Then measure the height of each person standing on tiptoes. Find the percent increase in height for each person, and determine if the increase is directly related to a person's foot length. Again, ask students to make predictions about the rank order of the percent increase before they make the measurements.

IN THE CLASSROOM   This activity is most appropriate for grades 7 and 8. Students at this level are consumers who nationally spend billions of dollars each year. Teachers can use many examples like those described above to make the concepts of the activity a real part of the students' world. Students at this age naturally love to challenge the adult world and find it "wrong." This aspect of the growing-up process can be exploited by the teacher who takes the time to present one or two examples of errors in advertising and then encourages students to find others. Students delight in finding such mistakes and then making them known to the advertiser or store owner — politely, of course!

• Activity

FLEX-IT

Body building for both men and women has been one of the fastest growing sports in the United States. In competition, contestants are judged on the muscle mass in the body and also on the increase in the size of various muscles as they are flexed. This is called muscle definition.

For this activity, consider that the members of the class are in a body building contest and that contestants are being judged on the basis of the percent increase in the bicep and calf muscles. Before making any measurements, write the names of each person in your group in the table below, and predict the rank order for the final percent increase for each muscle for each person. The highest rank is 1.

Take measurements as follows, and record them in the table:

A. Make all measurements in centimeters; round off to the nearest 0.5 cm.
B. Extend an arm, and measure the largest circumference of the bicep while it is fully relaxed.
C. Flex the arm as much as possible, and measure the largest circumference of the bicep muscle.
D. Extend a leg, and measure the largest circumference of the calf while it is fully relaxed.
E. Flex the leg as much as possible, and measure the largest circumference of the calf muscle.
F. Determine the percent increase for each muscle, and record it in the table.

Name	Bicep Extended	Bicep Flexed	Percent Increase	Rank Order of Increase	Calf Extended	Calf Flexed	Percent Increase	Rank Order of Increase

1. How does the final rank order of the percent increases compare with your predictions?

2. Did the most muscular person in your group have the greatest percent increase? _____ Explain.

3. What is the relationship between the person's size and the percent increase for those in your group?

4. Does the gender of a person affect the percent increase? _____ Explain.

III. TARGET NUMBER REVISITED

PURPOSE

This activity develops deeper understanding of the operations of decimal multiplication and division and develops skill with estimation of products and quotients.

MATERIALS

A calculator for each pair of students.

REQUIRED BACKGROUND

Students should:

• understand multiplication and division of decimals
• know the meaning of absolute value

TIME REQUIREMENT

30 to 40 minutes

GETTING STARTED

No special instruction is required; however, it may be helpful to explain the rules of the games and play a demonstration round with the class before the students play the games. Emphasize that the calculator may be used only to obtain the product or quotient as described in the rules. All computations involved in formulating guesses must be done mentally.

KEY IDEAS

Students often have the misconception that multiplying two positive numbers always results in a product that is greater than either of the factors, and, conversely, that division results in a quotient that is less than the dividend. In Game 1, students will often obtain a product that is greater than the target number. They must multiply by a number less than 1 to obtain a new product closer to the target number. Thus, the activity reinforces the concept that multiplication by a number less than 1 results in a product that is less than the greater factor. Similarly, in Game 2, when the dividend is less than the target quotient, the dividend must be divided by a number less than 1 to obtain a quotient that is greater than the dividend.

EXTENSIONS

If students have access to calculators that will perform the operations with common fractions, these games may be extended by playing them with common fractions instead of decimals.

IN THE CLASSROOM

These activities are appropriate for grades 6 through 8 to reinforce the operations of multiplication and division of decimals and fractions and to develop estimation skills. Initially, the acceptable range for a winning answer should be greater than that shown on the activity page. As students become familiar with the games and more proficient in making estimates, the range may be narrowed.

•Activity

TARGET NUMBER REVISITED

These are games for two players. Each pair will need one calculator.

GAME 1 Player 1 chooses the target product, and player 2 chooses a factor.
Then follow the steps in the flow chart.

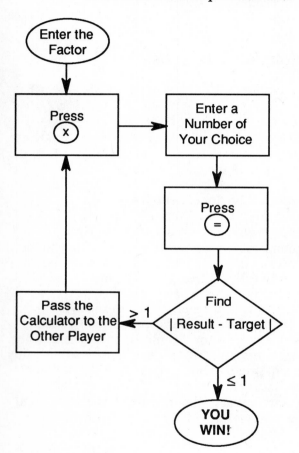

SAMPLE GAME
Target = 238   Factor = 9

Player	Keys Pressed	Display
1	9 (x) 15 (=)	135
2	(x) 1.4 (=)	189
1	(x) 1.2 (=)	226.8
2	(x) 1.05 (=)	238.14

Since | 238.14 - 238 | ≤ 1,
player 2 is the winner.

Try these games for practice.

Game	Target	Factor
1	585	15
2	1107	27
3	393	7
4	2139	13

Now make up some targets and factors
of your own.

GAME 2 Player 1 chooses the target quotient, and player 2 chooses the dividend.
Follow the steps in the flow chart above, but use the (÷) key in place of the
(x) key. *The result must be within 0.5 of the target to win.*

SAMPLE GAME
Target = 7   Dividend = 248

Player	Keys Pressed	Display
1	248 (÷) 25 (=)	9.92
2	(÷) 1.2 (=)	8.2666666
1	(÷) 1.17 (=)	7.065527

Since | 7.065527 - 7 | ≤ 0.5,
player 1 is the winner.

Try these games for practice.

Game	Target	Dividend
1	15	585
2	9	86
3	23	976
4	125	9

Now make up some targets and factors
of your own.

PROBABILITY

ACTIVITIES:
I. MONTE CARLO SIMULATIONS

I. MONTE CARLO SIMULATIONS

PURPOSE
These activities develop the use of Monte Carlo simulations for analyzing probability situations and simulating real world problems involving probability. They also develop a deeper understanding of the concepts of probability and the law of averages.

MATERIALS
For each student:

- a die
- a copy of the Random Digits Table (page 101)
- one computer per two or three students

REQUIRED BACKGROUND
Students should:

- understand the concept of the probability of an event
- understand the concept of independent events
- be able to compute the probability of independent events using a tree diagram
- be able to enter a computer program and execute it

TIME REQUIREMENT
- What's the Message?: 50 to 60 minutes
- An Airline's Dilemma: 110 to 120 minutes
- The Law of Averages: 50 to 60 minutes

GETTING STARTED
If students are familiar with the technique of Monte Carlo simulation, it is not essential to complete What's the Message? before doing An Airline's Dilemma. The Law of Averages may be done without completing either of the other activities; however, it may be beneficial to do What's the Message? first since information contained in it is referred to in The Law of Averages.

An Airline's Dilemma and The Law of Averages activities require use of a computer program called *MCSimulator*. The Monte Carlo Simulator pages (pages 106 to 108) provide a listing for the program. Before doing the activities, have someone enter the program and save it on a disk. Each student may then make a copy for personal use.

Students should work in groups of four or five to complete the activities. Explain that the activities involve a technique for constructing a model for a probability problem and conducting trials to estimate the answer. Since the solution depends on chance, the procedure is often called Monte Carlo simulation.

When using a table of random digits to conduct the trials, students should randomly select a starting point within the table and read the digits in order from that point until the desired number of trials is completed.

KEY IDEAS   The primary concept in these activities is that very complex problems from business, industry, and science that would normally require sophisticated mathematics can often be solved using simple methods. All that is required is a basic understanding of probabilities, independent events, and the concept popularly referred to as the law of averages.

WHAT'S THE MESSAGE? This activity develops a procedure for designing a Monte Carlo simulation. Problem 3 emphasizes the point that it is important to clearly identify any assumptions made in selecting the model if the model is to accurately describe the actual situation. In the example, we assume that 50 trials will be sufficient to determine an accurate estimate of the probability and that the probability of transmitting an erroneous data bit is independent of the results of the previous transmissions.

The problem is solved using two distinct types of probabilities. *Empirical probabilities* are determined by conducting a number of trials. Results of this type are found in problems 2, 8, and 9. Probabilities such as those in problem 5 that are determined by some method other than conducting trials are called mathematical or *a priori probabilities*.

In problems 2, 6, 7, 8, and 9, the question of how many trials are needed to obtain an accurate estimate of the probability is investigated by comparing the mathematical probability with empirical probabilities. As the number of trials is increased by combining results to obtain group and class totals, the experimental probability approaches the theoretical probability.

AN AIRLINE'S DILEMMA This activity extends the ideas in What's the Message? to a situation in which the mathematical probability cannot be readily calculated. A computer is used to conduct the simulation because the amount of time required to physically perform the number of trials necessary to obtain accurate results would be prohibitive.

The activity also illustrates the connection between probability and statistics. Airlines use statistical methods to determine what proportion of people holding confirmed reservations will show up for a flight as well as the average value of a free ticket issued to compensate a passenger who is denied a seat. Probability theory is then applied to the statistical data to maximize the income from each flight by overbooking.

In problem 14, it is important to consider other variables in addition to the amount of reduction in income when deciding on an overbooking policy. If airlines turn away too many passengers by overbooking, their public relations image will be affected. Before establishing an overbooking policy, airlines might do a statistical study on how the average number of standby passengers is related to the number of confirmed reservations made. If airlines can count on having three or four standby passengers for each flight, then they can reduce the number of reservations needed to maximize their income from each flight by three or four and, in the process, reduce the possibility of having to deny boarding to a passenger with a reservation.

Since the number of reservations must be a whole number, the data plotted in the graph preceding problem 12 are a discrete set, not a continuous set. Strictly speaking, then, it is inappropriate to connect the data points with a smooth curve as the students were instructed to do. Although a continuous curve does not accurately model the problem, it does make it easier to obtain a clear picture of how the amount of income reduction varies with the number of confirmed reservations.

Probabilities are usually expressed as simple ratios or fractions, but probabilities and ratios are really not the same thing. Problems 1, 9, and 10 illustrate this distinction. In problem 1, a simple ratio is used to show that, if 126 reservations are made for a flight, then exactly 105 passengers will show up for it. However, in problems 9 and 10, where the ratio is interpreted as a probability, we find that, when 126 reservations are made, fewer than 105 people show up for some flights and more than 105 show up for others. Unlike a simple ratio, a probability cannot produce an exact result in a specific case; it can only predict what will happen "on an average" in a large number of identical cases. This distinction has given rise to the popularly held notion of a law of averages.

THE LAW OF AVERAGES The mathematical analogy of the law of averages is the law of large numbers. The problems in The Law of Averages activity explore some of the implications of the law of large numbers and how these implications are often misinterpreted. Problem 19 develops the most familiar implication of the law of large numbers: if the probability of an event is p, then, as the number of trials increases, the ratio of the number of times the event occurs to the total number of trials approaches p. This idea is often misinterpreted as meaning that, as the number of trials increases, the actual number of times the event occurs approaches the expected number. However, problem 20 shows that, as the number of trials increases, it is possible for the difference between the actual and expected values to get larger.

Problem 18 illustrates the fact that, for small numbers of trials, the empirical probabilities can vary greatly from the actual probability. This principle explains why it is not unusual to get eight heads in succession when tossing a fair coin, even though the probability of it happening is very small. Problem 17 demonstrates that, as the number of tosses increases, it becomes more likely that a long string of heads or tails will occur.

EXTENSIONS The activities may be extended by having each student pose a problem that can be solved using a Monte Carlo simulation and then doing the simulation. *The Art and Techniques of Simulation* and *Exploring Probability* in the Quantitative Literacy Series published by Dale Seymour Publications also include a variety of interesting activities and problems to extend the concepts presented here.

IN THE CLASSROOM These activities are appropriate for students in grades 7 and 8. The material preceding problem 1 of What's the Message? should be presented orally. An Airline's Dilemma should be separated into two activities, the first part ending with problem 8.

•Activity

WHAT'S THE MESSAGE?

The telemetry system aboard a spacecraft transmits data and pictures back to a tracking station on Earth. The telemetry signals are in the form of pulses imposed on a radio wave. Since the absence of a pulse may be read as a 0 and the presence of a pulse as a 1, the telemetry signals may be interpreted as binary digits. A binary digit, a 0 or a 1, is called a bit.

Example:

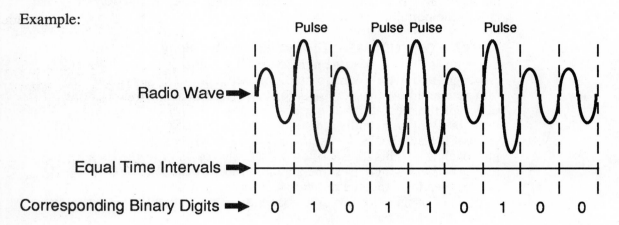

Radio Wave ➡

Equal Time Intervals ➡

Corresponding Binary Digits ➡   0   1   0   1   1   0   1   0   0

Equipment malfunctions can cause a 0 to be transmitted as a 1, and vice versa. Let us assume that the telemetry system aboard one spacecraft has a 10% probability of transmitting an erroneous bit. To increase the reliability of the data received from this spacecraft, each message bit is repeated three times in the transmission.

Example:

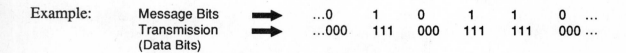

Message Bits   ➡   ...0   1   0   1   1   0 ...
Transmission   ➡   ...000 111 000 111 111 000 ...
(Data Bits)

When a transmission is received at the Earth station, each successive triplet of bits in the transmission is converted back to a single message bit. Since the triplets 000, 100, 010, and 001 probably contain at most one transmission error, they are all converted to a 0. Similarly, the triplets 111, 110, 101, and 011 are all converted to a 1.

We want to determine the probability that a message bit transmitted using this coding process will be incorrect when interpreted at the Earth station. To find the answer, we can simulate the problem as follows.

Step 1: Select a model

Since the probability of a data bit transmitted from the spacecraft being incorrect is 10%, we will model the transmission of a single data bit by selecting one digit from a table of random digits. If the digit selected is a 0, an erroneous data bit is transmitted. If the digit selected is any of the digits 1 through 9, the correct data bit is transmitted.

Step 2: Define a trial

Since each message bit is repeated three times in the transmission, a trial consists of selecting three successive digits from a table of random digits. Each random digit selected from the table indicates whether the respective data bit in the triplet is transmitted correctly or not. At the Earth station, the triplet will be converted to an incorrect message bit if two or three of the individual data bits are transmitted incorrectly. Thus, if the trial contains two or three 0's, the message bit will be interpreted incorrectly.

Step 3: Conduct a trial and record the result

Example: The *observation of interest* or *result* is the number of erroneous data bits that were transmitted. This result is determined by the number of 0's in the trial.

	TRIAL	RESULT		CONCLUSION
Trial A ➡	408	1	second data bit incorrect	Message bit is correct.
Trial B ➡	661	0	no data bits incorrect	Message bit is correct.
Trial C ➡	010	2	first and third data bits incorrect	Message bit is incorrect.

1. Complete 50 trials, and record the results in the table:

TRIAL	RESULT	TRIAL	RESULT	TRIAL	RESULT	TRIAL	RESULT	TRIAL	RESULT
1 ___	___	11 ___	___	21 ___	___	31 ___	___	41 ___	___
2 ___	___	12 ___	___	22 ___	___	32 ___	___	42 ___	___
3 ___	___	13 ___	___	23 ___	___	33 ___	___	43 ___	___
4 ___	___	14 ___	___	24 ___	___	34 ___	___	44 ___	___
5 ___	___	15 ___	___	25 ___	___	35 ___	___	45 ___	___
6 ___	___	16 ___	___	26 ___	___	36 ___	___	46 ___	___
7 ___	___	17 ___	___	27 ___	___	37 ___	___	47 ___	___
8 ___	___	18 ___	___	28 ___	___	38 ___	___	48 ___	___
9 ___	___	19 ___	___	29 ___	___	39 ___	___	49 ___	___
10 ___	___	20 ___	___	30 ___	___	40 ___	___	50 ___	___

Step 4: Interpret the results

The probability that a message bit will be incorrect is determined by dividing the number of trials with two or more 0's by the total number of trials.

2. a. Based on your 50 trials, what is the probability that a message bit will be incorrect? _____

   b. Do you believe the result is an accurate estimate of the probability? Explain.

3. What assumptions were made in designing this simulation?

4. What are the advantages and disadvantages of using the coding process described above for transmitting telemetry data?

5. A tree diagram for the telemetry problem has been started below. Complete the diagram, and use it to compute the probability that a message bit will be incorrect.

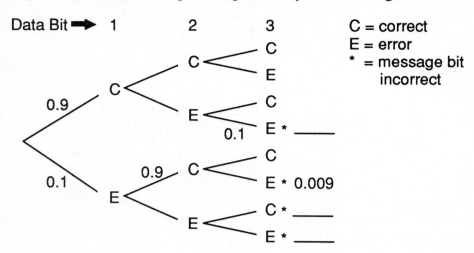

6. How does the probability you computed in problem 5 compare with your result in problem 2?

7. How could you improve your result in problem 2?

Enter the results of your experiment in the table below. Then combine your results with those of the other members of your group to complete the Group column in the table.

	Individual	Group	Class
Number of Trials			
Number with Two or More Zeroes			
Probability Message Bit Is Incorrect			

8. How does the probability determined using the group data compare with the probability you computed in problem 5?

9. Now combine your group data with the data for the other groups in the class, and complete the Class column in the table. How does the probability determined using the class data compare with the probability you computed in problem 5?

RANDOM DIGITS TABLE

28347	36646	92715	62062	24242	04651	77553	26207	04121	38254
93711	70034	10940	32402	62429	33925	77585	99423	78020	03989
58713	66613	78692	89594	77622	69992	11410	95103	50976	01268
77589	22566	93883	83655	18386	38846	54633	72863	40241	65718
88625	84024	54074	53284	96271	36675	27908	34242	30755	38840
32770	66912	39682	98005	52935	24871	62843	98057	23451	80631
47110	01460	24515	94293	47775	59011	65605	66501	60570	06204
22903	13150	24523	94473	66579	38357	51757	54972	85256	13303
89151	93397	83721	26048	80547	33178	67906	36532	61581	37318
43457	41807	65383	49386	66158	37044	18601	19097	81958	96398
01733	94346	76039	99652	85304	95792	41871	99026	61055	26062
15770	09857	68553	21006	63276	27283	37005	42314	27564	88713
31810	10309	03083	28852	61704	68653	80113	43824	31671	29017
60365	00143	55426	96602	71883	10549	77581	13486	15884	24980
23030	19420	23285	51986	94278	17513	33298	44205	39394	98131
65917	82529	12015	38163	85908	11730	15418	84121	48045	00829
42192	40334	84640	70143	31024	42543	48758	29868	36771	25068
10730	55392	72470	16425	23315	47386	88130	57075	99118	66077
77237	38035	06629	80244	20243	46536	98613	02906	22070	25811
28260	93771	86635	36119	95359	52348	62899	56503	53599	38318
61458	21195	69067	75157	07220	29173	01810	81115	21862	13728
89304	11733	01337	35385	89000	65896	57512	61690	28407	64140
38034	20621	30319	14383	41966	92077	85587	11625	92264	37565
39927	43463	51058	62096	78576	60331	78919	19779	06886	36720
43460	44927	98507	02955	26570	09854	58533	39807	20269	09792
45911	40462	15925	01298	26883	45091	32362	13843	99466	27456
20725	42440	48827	28650	02775	76673	20388	75089	37443	52708
69402	82502	17836	79424	29935	13549	69420	33796	46190	47265
52017	84597	02505	33077	35993	26271	54866	08008	32236	12683
41949	91807	57883	65394	35595	39198	75268	40336	50658	32089
78007	58644	73823	62854	31151	64726	88795	93736	22189	47004
48304	77410	78871	98387	44647	12807	65194	58586	78232	57097
01430	00304	32036	23671	62932	99837	20160	27792	37090	62165
11172	66827	39830	04587	64810	25649	56530	94864	78584	38417
68359	90072	49513	56420	77661	86284	13593	09065	83538	89003
17811	71285	13453	08563	28517	38258	88759	35279	91930	88216
12842	23549	77521	03874	59673	50111	63607	46699	62241	11033
50334	36475	81615	41959	13899	87026	68035	05839	72234	40065
24052	95658	98335	21125	45364	67989	32451	63412	72427	76558
28958	64526	06159	21150	45287	02833	20565	20846	63664	72162
75338	04022	77166	83339	99021	18090	91809	09799	75883	36480
37067	40933	65634	79883	11519	97203	70899	00697	84864	24470
07933	48202	15392	44976	31092	75226	43915	45473	59179	53276
00281	77819	58762	85104	13791	21939	09499	22885	17969	43752
95845	99396	37855	64823	83865	40471	69119	62786	36389	38045

•Activity

AN AIRLINE'S DILEMMA

An airline has determined that one-sixth of all passengers holding confirmed reservations fail to show up for their flight. To avoid partially filled flights, the airline has resorted to overbooking flights, that is, selling more tickets than there are seats on the plane.

1. The airline's fleet consists entirely of 105-passenger Boeing 737-100 aircraft. If five-sixths of the passengers holding confirmed reservations for a flight show up, how many reservations should the airline make for a flight to have a full flight but not have to turn away any passengers with reservations? _____ Explain.

The airline has adopted the policy of confirming a maximum of 126 reservations on any of its flights. After 126 reservations have been made, passengers who want to take a chance that there will be seats available are placed on a standby list. You are the first passenger on the standby list for a flight on which 126 people hold confirmed reservations. Complete the following problems to estimate the probability that you will get a seat on the flight.

2. Describe how a die could be used to model whether a passenger holding a confirmed reservation shows up for the flight or not.

3. Describe a trial for the simulation.

4. What is the observation of interest?

5. Conduct one trial by rolling a die. Record and interpret the result.

Completing this simulation by physically rolling a die to complete 100 trials is very time consuming and subject to recording errors. For these reasons, a computer is usually used to conduct the trials in a Monte Carlo simulation. The following problems illustrate this process.

We will *model* whether or not a person holding a confirmed reservation on the flight shows up for it by selecting a random digit from 1 through 6. Since 5 of every 6 people holding a reservation show up, we will let the digits 1 through 5 represent the cases where the person shows up for the flight, and the digit 6 will represent the cases where the person does not.

Since 126 people have reservations, a *trial* will consist of selecting 126 random digits. If a trial contains fewer than 105 of the digits 1 through 5 (that is, fewer than 105 of the people holding reservations show up for the flight), then you get a seat on the plane, and the trial is considered a *success*.

Run the program *MCSimulator*. When the computer displays each instruction,
respond by performing the indicated action.

COMPUTER DISPLAY	**ACTION**

ENTER INFORMATION FOR THE MODEL

    USE NUMBERS 1 THROUGH ?   **Enter 6. This instructs the computer to select random digits 1 through 6.**

    DIGITS OF INTEREST: 1 - ?   **Enter 5. This tells the computer that a digit 1 through 5 means the person shows up for the flight.**

ENTER INFORMATION FOR A TRIAL

    LENGTH: HOW MANY NUMBERS?   **Since a trial consists of selecting 126 random digits (one for each person holding a reservation), enter 126.**

    NUMBER OF TRIALS?   **Enter 100.**

OBSERVATION OF INTEREST:

    NO.OF SUCCESSES IS (<,>,=) TO —?   **We want to know if fewer than 105 people with reservations show up for the flight, so press < (don't forget to hold down the SHIFT key).**
    ENTER SYMBOL

    ENTER NUMBER   **Enter 105.**

It takes some time for the computer to complete 100 trials, so be patient.
Record the output in the Individual column in the table.

	Individual	Group	Class
Number of Trials			
Number of Successes			
Probability of Getting a Seat			

6.   Combine your results with those obtained by the other members of your group, and complete the Group column in the table. How does the probability determined using the group data compare with the individual probability?

7.   Now combine your group data with the data from the other groups in the class, and complete the Class column in the table. How does the probability determined using the class data compare with the individual and group probabilities?

8.   What would you estimate your probability of getting a seat on the flight to be? _____

The airline's income from each flight is reduced if the flight is not full, but the airline's overbooking policy can also result in reduced income. Federal law requires that, when passengers holding confirmed reservations for a flight are denied boarding because the flight is overbooked, the airline must pay them "denied boarding compensation." Denied boarding compensation usually means providing the passengers with seats on the next available flight to their destination as well as giving them a free round trip ticket to any destination that the airline serves in the contiguous 48 states. ·

The following problems explore how a simulation could be used to maximize the income from each flight. Before proceeding, make the following modifications to the *MCSimulator* program:

```
180  TS = 0: ES = 0: DP = 0
260  IF SUCCESS < TEST THEN ES = ES + TEST - SUCCESS
270  IF SUCCESS > TEST THEN DP = DP + SUCCESS - TEST
370  PRINT"EMPTY SEATS = ";ES
380  PRINT"FREE TICKETS = ";DP
```

These modifications enable the program to keep track of the number of empty seats on partially filled flights and the number of free tickets given away because of overbooking.

Run the program using the same input as before. Use the results to answer the following questions:

9. If the airline makes 126 confirmed reservations for every flight, on an average, how many free tickets will they give away per flight? Hint: Each trial represents one flight.

10. On an average, how many empty seats will they have per flight?

11. The airline has determined that their income from a particular flight is reduced by $124.00 for each empty seat on the flight and by $398.00 for every free ticket they must give away. Why does a free ticket reduce income more than an empty seat on a flight?

Use your answers to problems 9 and 10 and the airline's data for the values of free tickets and empty seats in problem 11 to complete the column for 126 confirmed reservations in the following table.

No. of Confirmed Reservations		105	110	120	122	124	126	128	130		
Empty Seats	No. per Flight										
	Cost										
Free Tickets	No. per Flight										
	Cost										
Amount Income Is Reduced											

Use the *MCSimulator* program to determine the number of empty seats and the number of free tickets per flight for each number of confirmed reservations in the table on the preceding page. Run 100 trials for each number of reservations. Complete the remaining entries in each column, and then plot the data points on the graph below.

To get a clearer picture of how the amount of income reduction varies with the number of confirmed reservations, draw a smooth curve connecting the data points. It may be necessary to run the program for numbers of reservations other than those in the table to get a more accurate graph.

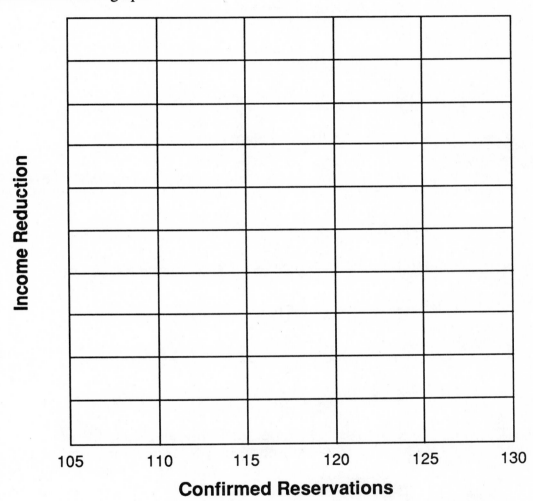

12. Based on your graph, predict the number of confirmed reservations for which the reduction in income is the least. _____

13. By how much will the income per flight be reduced? _____

Check your results by running the program and using your prediction in problem 12 for the length of a trial. Record the results in the table on page 104.

14. If you were running the airline, what overbooking policy would you adopt?
    Explain your reasons for choosing the policy.

MONTE CARLO SIMULATOR

Monte Carlo Simulator is an example of a program that may be used to generate data for a Monte Carlo simulation. The program is written for use on Apple computers, but it may be easily modified for use on other computers.

Enter the program as listed on the next page, and then test it. When the computer displays each instruction, respond by performing the indicated action.

COMPUTER DISPLAY	ACTION
ENTER INFORMATION FOR THE MODEL	
USE NUMBERS 1 THROUGH ?	**Enter 2. This instructs the computer to select random digits 1 or 2.**
DIGITS OF INTEREST: 1 - ?	**Enter 1. This tells the computer that the digit 1 means the desired event occurred, that is, the probability that it will occur is 0.5.**
ENTER INFORMATION FOR A TRIAL	
LENGTH: HOW MANY NUMBERS?	**Enter 4. This means a trial consists of selecting four random digits.**
NUMBER OF TRIALS?	**Enter 80.**
OBSERVATION OF INTEREST:	
NO.OF SUCCESSES IS (<,>,=) TO —?	
ENTER SYMBOL	**Press the = key.**
ENTER NUMBER	**Enter 2. These entries tell the computer to count the number of trials containing 2 ones.**

If the program is working correctly, the output should have the form

# TRIALS	# SUC.	P(SUC.)
80	X	Y

where X and Y are *approximately* 30 and 0.375, respectively.

If necessary, debug the program. When it is working correctly, save it as *MCSimulator*. The program will be used in several activities and referred to by this name.

PROGRAM LISTING

```
10   HOME
20   PRINT"ENTER INFORMATION FOR THE
       MODEL:"
30   PRINT
40   INPUT"   USE NUMBERS 1 THROUGH ?
       ";LD
50   INPUT"   DIGITS OF INTEREST: 1 -
       ? ";S
60   PRINT
70   GOSUB 600
80   PRINT"OBSERVATION OF INTEREST:"
90   PRINT
100  PRINT"  NO. OF SUCCESSES IS (<,
     >,=) TO —?"
110  PRINT"   ENTER SYMBOL ";
120  GET SY$
130  IF SY$="<" OR SY$=">" OR SY$="=
     " THEN 150
140  GOTO 120
150  PRINT SY$
160  INPUT"   ENTER NUMBER ";TEST
170  PRINT
180  TS=0
190  FOR TRIAL = 1 TO NT
200  SUCCESS = O
210  FOR DIGIT = 1 TO ND
220  RDIGIT = INT(LD*RND(1))+1
230  IF RDIGIT > S THEN 250
240  SUCCESS = SUCCESS + 1
250  NEXT DIGIT

290  IF SY$ = "<" AND SUCCESS < TEST
       THEN TS = TS + 1
300  IF SY$ = ">" AND SUCCESS > TEST
       THEN TS = TS + 1
310  IF SY$ = "=" AND SUCCESS = TEST
       THEN TS = TS + 1
330  NEXT TRIAL
340  PRINT"# TRIALS", "# SUC.", "P(S
     UC.)"
350  PRINT NT, TS, INT(1000*TS/NT +
       .5)/1000
400  PRINT
410  PRINT
420  PRINT"RUN PROGRAM AGAIN? ";
430  GET A$
440  IF A$ = "N" THEN 550
450  IF A$ <> "Y" THEN 430
460  HOME
470  PRINT"ENTER 1 TO CHANGE ALL DAT
     A,"
```

Lines 10 through 170 contain the input routines for entering the data for the model, the number of trials and the observation of interest.

Line 180 initializes the counter. The loop in lines 190 through 330 repeats the desired number of trials. The loop in lines 210 through 250 selects a random number in the range 1 through LD and checks to see if it represents a success.

Lines 290 through 310 count the number of trials meeting the conditions for the observation of interest.

Lines 340 and 350 output results.

Lines 400 through 550 allow user to rerun the program or to end the program.

```
480 PRINT"OR 2 TO CHANGE JUST TRIAL
      DATA.";
490 GET A$
500 IF A$ = "1" THEN 10
510 IF A$ <> "2" THEN 490
520 HOME
530 GOSUB 600
540 GOTO 180
550 END
600 PRINT"ENTER INFORMATION FOR A
      TRIAL:"
610 PRINT
620 INPUT"  LENGTH: HOW MANY NUMBER
    S? ";ND
630 INPUT"  NUMBER OF TRIALS? ";NT
640 PRINT
650 RETURN
```

The subroutine from line 600 through line 650 allows entry of data for a trial.

• **Looking Back**

THE LAW OF AVERAGES

The number of boys and the number of girls born in this hospital each day are usually different, but over a long period of time the number of male births and the number of female births will be equal.

She's had eight heads in a row tossing that coin. The next toss has to be a tail!

You have probably heard numerous statements like the ones above. Their truth is often attributed to one of the more frequently misunderstood concepts in mathematics, the law of averages. This activity explores the law of averages and what it implies.

In the activity, the *MCSimulator* program will be used to simulate the data coding problem from the What's the Message? activity. Before proceeding, load the program, and make the following modifications to it. The modifications instruct the computer to find the longest sequence of correct message bits occurring in any trial.

```
180  TS=0: T=0: MF=0: F=0
320  GOSUB 700
360  PRINT"LONGEST STRING OF CORRECT"
370  PRINT"MESSAGE BITS = ";MF
700  IF TS=T THEN 740
710  IF F>MF THEN MF=F
720  F=0: T=TS
730  GOTO 750
740  F=F+1
750  RETURN
```

Refer to the data transmission problem in What's the Message? and run the program. When the computer displays each instruction, respond by performing the indicated action.

COMPUTER DISPLAY	**ACTION**
ENTER INFORMATION FOR THE MODEL	
USE NUMBERS 1 THROUGH ?	**Enter 10. Select random digits 1 through 10.**
DIGITS OF INTEREST: 1 - ?	**Enter 1. The digit 1 means an erroneous data bit was transmitted.**
ENTER INFORMATION FOR A TRIAL	
LENGTH: HOW MANY NUMBERS?	**Enter 3. Each message bit is repeated 3 times.**
NUMBER OF TRIALS?	**Enter 250.**
OBSERVATION OF INTEREST:	
NO.OF SUCCESSES IS (<,>,=) TO —?	**The message bit is incorrect if the trial contains 2 or 3 ones, so press the > key.**
ENTER NUMBER	**Enter 1.**

Record the output in the first row of the table below. The number of incorrect message bits should be recorded in the Actual column.

15. In What's the Message? a tree diagram was used to show that the probability that a message bit is translated incorrectly is 0.028. How many incorrect message bits would you expect to have in the 250 trials? Record your answer in the Expected column in the table.

16. What is the *absolute value* of the difference between the actual number of incorrect message bits and the expected number? Record your answer in the Difference column.

Repeat the simulation for each number of trials listed in the table. Record the output of the program in the appropriate columns. Then compute the expected number of incorrect message bits and the absolute value of the difference between the actual and expected numbers. Record all the answers in the table.

Number of Trials	Number of Incorrect Message Bits			Probability Message Bit Is Incorrect	Longest String of Correct Message Bits
	Expected	Actual	Difference		
250					
500					
750					
1000					
2000					
3000					
4000					
5000					

17. As the number of trials increases, what appears to happen to the longest string of correct message bits?

Construct a line graph for the number of trials and the probability that a message bit is incorrect on the axes below. The broken line on the grid represents the theoretical probability of 0.028.

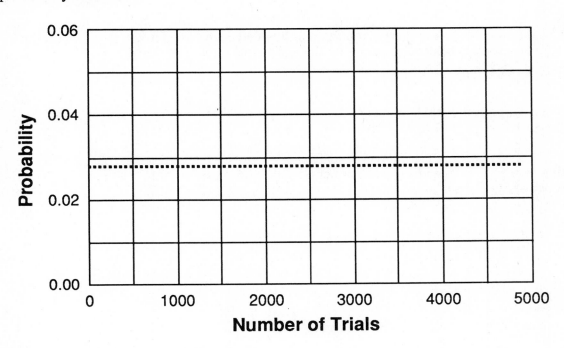

18. When the number of trials is between 1 and 1000, what can you conclude about the variation in the probabilities?

19. What happens to the probabilities as the number of trials increases?

20. Examine the data in the Difference column of the table. Is it true that, as the probability of an incorrect message bit gets closer to 0.028, the actual number of incorrect bits gets closer to the expected number of incorrect bits? Explain.

21. Use your observations from problems 18 through 20 to answer the following questions. Assume that the probabilities of a male birth and a female birth are both 0.5.

   a. An average of ten children are born in a particular hospital each day. How will the number of male births compare with the number of female births each day?

   b. Over a five-year period, what happens to the ratio of the total number of male births to the total number of female births?

   c. Over a five-year period, does the total number of male births get closer to the total number of female births? Explain.

   d. Contrast the answers to parts a through c with the first statement at the beginning of the activity.

22. Use your observations from problems 17 and 18 to answer the following questions. Assume that the coin in question is a fair one.

   a. A coin was tossed eight times and came up heads each time. Does this contradict the law of averages? Why or why not?

   b. A coin was tossed 197 times. The last eight tosses came up heads. Does this contradict the law of averages? Why or why not?

   c. In either of the preceding problems, what is the probability that the next toss of the coin will come up heads?

EXPLORING DATA

ACTIVITIES:
I. WHAT'S THE AVERAGE?
II. STATISTICS WITH "M&M'S"®
III. THE WEATHER REPORT

I. WHAT'S THE AVERAGE?

PURPOSE This activity provides a concrete introduction to the measures of central tendency, mean, median, and mode, and it examines how each of the averages is affected by extremes in the data.

MATERIALS 15 strips of 1-centimeter grid paper for each group of two or three students.

TIME REQUIREMENT 30 to 40 minutes

GETTING STARTED No special instruction is necessary, but the strips of grid paper (13 to 15 squares per strip) should be cut in advance. Students should work in groups of two or three to reduce the amount of time spent labeling the strips.

KEY IDEAS This activity focuses on the meanings of mean, median, and mode, and discusses:

- how each measure provides an indication of where data are centered or concentrated
- how each measure is affected by extremes in the data (that is, unusually large or small data points or the occurrence of one data point with unusually high frequency)
- how the physical modeling in the activity is related to the algorithm for computing the average

Problem 3 develops the concept of the mean. It illustrates that the mean has a leveling or smoothing effect on the data. Another way of expressing this is, if all the data had the same value, the data points would all equal the mean. When data are "reasonably well behaved," the mean is near the center of the data and close to the region of greatest concentration of data. The mean is the most commonly used average – in fact, most people erroneously use the terms *average* and *mean* synonymously. However, as shown in problems 6 and 7, the value of the mean may be affected by extremes in the data, and therefore, it may not be the most representative value to use for an average. Problem 12 extends the concrete process used for determining the mean in the preceding problems to the computational algorithm.

Problem 1 develops the concept of the median. Problem 4 demonstrates that the value of the median is not significantly affected by unusually large or small data points, thus illustrating that the median is a more appropriate average than the mean when there are extremes in the data. However, the median may not accurately reflect concentrations in the data, as is shown in problems 8 and 11.

When data are "reasonably well behaved," they tend to cluster around the mode. In this sense, the mode is a measure of where the data are concentrated. Its usefulness is limited, however, since the frequency of occurrence of the mode may not be significantly different than that of other data points, the mode may be an outlier, or the data may have more than one mode. Problem 11 illustrates these considerations.

Students may use the following reasoning to answer problem 13:

- The average given is an actual shoe size. This would be unlikely to happen if the mean were calculated. The average is also one of the smaller sizes, which would seem to indicate that it is the mode rather than the median.

- The mode would be a whole number, and the median would either be a whole number or a number of the form $x.5$, where x is a whole number. Thus, the average, 2.67, must be the mean.

- The mean probably would be higher because of the extremely high salaries of some corporate executives, entertainers, and sports figures, and the mode would most likely be a number like 28,000 rather than 28,236.

These arguments are valid. However, to determine which average would be the most appropriate for the given data, it is more important to reason in terms of the nature of the data and which average provides the best indication of where the data are centered or concentrated. The answers provided reflect this type of reasoning.

EXTENSIONS

Students should investigate the effect on the three averages produced by adding a constant to each data point or by multiplying each data point by a constant. For example, to investigate the effect of adding a constant, students could compute the three averages for the lengths of the names of Alaska, Alabama, Arizona, Colorado, Delaware, Florida, Washington, Tennessee, and Mississippi and compare them with their answers for problems 1 through 3.

Students should also find examples of the use of averages in the media. They should determine which average was used and explain why they believe it is or is not appropriate, based on the nature of the data it summarizes. If the average is not appropriate, they should also discuss the bias the user is supporting by citing it as the average.

IN THE CLASSROOM

This activity may be used in grades 4 through 7 to introduce or to reinforce the concept of an average and the use of the mean, median, and mode. Computation of the mean is often taught in isolation as an application of division and is referred to as finding the average. As a result, students develop an incomplete understanding of the mean and are left with the impression that it is the only measure of central tendency. This activity addresses these deficiencies by introducing the three measures of central tendency simultaneously and by focusing on the concept of an average and the interpretation of the mean, median, and mode.

•Activity

WHAT'S THE AVERAGE?

When describing a set of data, it is often convenient to use a single number that indicates where the data are centered or concentrated. Such a number is often called the *average*. The mean, the median, and the mode are three commonly used averages.

A. Write the name of each of the following states on a strip of graph paper. Use one strip of paper for each state and one square for each letter in the name.

Arizona, Hawaii, Ohio, Maine, Oregon, Idaho, Texas, Louisiana, Kentucky.

B. Arrange the names from shortest to longest, as shown in the example at the right.

N	E	V	A	D	A
M	O	N	T	A	N	A
V	I	R	G	I	N	I	A
W	I	S	C	O	N	S	I	N
M	I	N	N	E	S	O	T	A

THE MEDIAN

1. a. What is the middle state in the list? _____
(If there is no middle state, find the two center states.)

   In the example, the middle state is Virginia.

   b. How many letters are in its name? _____
(If there is no middle state, add the number of letters in the names of the two center states, and divide by 2.)

   This is the *median* length for the names of the states. In the example, the median is 8.

Median ➡

N	E	V	A	D	A
M	O	N	T	A	N	A
V	I	R	G	I	N	I	A
W	I	S	C	O	N	S	I	N
M	I	N	N	E	S	O	T	A

THE MODE

2. Examine the names in the list. What number of letters occurs most often in the names of the states? _____

   This is the *mode* of the lengths of the names of the states. In the example, the mode is 9.

Mode {

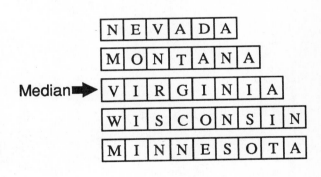

THE MEAN

To find the mean of the lengths of the names, cut off letters from the longer names and move them to fill in the shorter ones. Continue cutting off and moving letters until all the rows have as close to the same number of letters as possible.

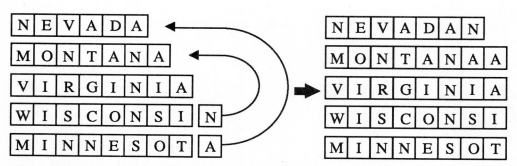

The mean in this example is a little less than 8 because all the rows except one contain eight letters.

3.   What is the *mean* of the lengths of the names of the nine states? _____

Write each letter of *Massachusetts* in a square on a strip of graph paper. Add this to the data for the other nine states, and repeat the steps for determining the median, mode, and mean.

4.   The median of the lengths of the names of the ten states is _____.

5.   The mode is _____.

6.   The mean is _____.

7.   Compare these results with those derived for the original nine states. Describe how the addition of *Massachusetts* affected the mean, median, and mode, and explain the differences.

Remove the data for *Massachusetts*. Write the names *Maryland, Michigan,* and *Oklahoma* on strips of graph paper. Add them to the data for the original nine states, and repeat the steps for determining the median, mode, and mean.

8.   The median of the lengths of the names of the twelve states is _____.

9.   The mode is _____.

10.   The mean is _____.

11.   Compare these results with those derived for the original nine states. Describe how these additions affected the mean, median, and mode, and explain the differences.

12. To find the mean of the lengths of the names of n states, the letters making up the names of the states must be separated into n equal (or nearly equal) sets. Explain how this could be done without writing each letter on a square.

13. Which average, mean, median, or mode, do you think was used in each of the following statements? Explain your choice in each case.

   a. The average lady's shoe size is 7½. _____

   b. The average size of a household in the United States is 2.67 people. _____

   c. The average annual family income in the United States is $28,236. _____

14. Sam Slugger's contract with the Columbus Mudcats baseball team says that his annual salary will be $1,000,000 times the average of his batting averages for the preceding five seasons. Sam's batting averages for the past five seasons were .145, .130, .160, .130, and .495.

   a. If you were Sam, which average, mean, median, or mode, would you want to use to compute your salary? _____ Why?

   b. If you were the general manager of the Mudcats, which average would you want to use? _____ Why?

   c. Sam's contract went to arbitration. You are the arbitrator. Which average would you use to compute Sam's salary, and how would you justify your decision?

II. STATISTICS WITH "M&M'S"®[1]

PURPOSE   This activity introduces the use of sampling to predict population characteristics. Students also learn how to construct real graphs, pictographs, line plots, frequency tables, and bar graphs and to interpret the data presented in them.

MATERIALS   For each class:

- a one-pound bag of "M&M's"® Plain Chocolate Candies
- a one-tablespoon measuring spoon
- a beam balance or a balance scale and weights
- 6 line plot charts, one for each color of "M&M's"® (page 127)
- 6 frequency tables, one for each color of "M&M's"® (page 127)
- 1 Favorite Color frequency table (page 128)
- a calculator for each student

REQUIRED BACKGROUND   Students should know how to construct a bar graph.

TIME REQUIREMENT   70 to 80 minutes

GETTING STARTED   This activity should be done as a whole class activity. Prior to class, make six copies of the tables for "M&M's"® (page 127) containing the line plot and frequency table charts and one copy of page 128 containing the Favorite Color chart. Label each line plot and each frequency table with one of the six colors. Establish six recording stations, each with the two charts for a single color, at different locations around the room. The Favorite Color chart should be placed at a seventh station. Place the bag of "M&M's"® , the measuring spoon, and the scale and weights at the front of the room, where students will have easy access to them.

Divide the class into six groups. After all students have entered the data for their samples on the charts, give each group the line plot chart and frequency table for one of the colors. Each group should use the charts to determine the total number of "M&M's"® of that color in the samples and report it to the rest of the class. The totals from the Favorite Color chart should also be reported to the class.

KEY IDEAS   The focus of this activity is on the potential uses and limitations of each statistical display, not just on the construction of each display.

In general, real graphs do not provide a practical method for displaying statistical data. Pictographs are common in the popular media, probably because of their aesthetic appeal. However, the symbol used is often an irregular shape, making it difficult to accurately divide the symbol into fractional parts or to identify precisely what fractional part appears in the display. These difficulties make pictographs hard to interpret and construct. Bar graphs, however, display exactly the same information, and they have the advantage of being easy to construct and interpret.

Because line plots are quick and easy to construct, they provide a very useful tool for preliminary data analysis. Maximum and minimum values, clusters and gaps in the data, outliers (data points that are extremely large

1. "M&M's"® is a registered trademark of Mars, Incorporated.

or small in comparison with the rest of the data), the median, and modes are all easily identified on a line plot. The major limitation is that line plots are convenient to use only with relatively small sets of data.

Frequency tables provide a very useful means for tabulating data. Maximum and minimum values, the median, and modes are easily identified in a frequency table, but clusters and gaps in the data and outliers are not as easily identified.

Predicting the characteristics of a population from a sample is an important concept in statistics. The reliability of such predictions is affected by two factors, the sample size and the randomness of the sample. Problems 6, 7, 11, and 12 develop the idea that, in general, assuming that the samples are selected randomly, predictions become more accurate as the size of the sample increases. It should also be apparent that, depending on the size of the population, there is some point at which taking a larger sample will result only in minimal changes in the predictions.

The idea of randomness is demonstrated by the fact that there is a great deal of variation in the individual samples. One possible explanation for this might be that the number of "M&M's"® Plain Chocolate Candies of any one color varies at different depths in the bag. Similarly, the number of people who prefer a particular color of "M&M's"® may vary by group or by region in the country. For this reason, the manufacturer probably would not use the data from problem 13 since a class of university students is not a random sample of all "M&M's"® eaters.

EXTENSIONS

The activity may be extended by repeating it using a mixture consisting of one pound each of lima, pinto, kidney, and black beans. Because the sizes of the beans vary, students may predict that the smallest bean will occur most often in their sample and the largest bean will occur least often.

If it is possible to share results of the activity with classes in other geographical regions or to obtain bags of "M&M's"® purchased in other regions, an interesting extension is to try to determine whether there are regional differences in the compositions of bags of "M&M's"® and, if so, to explain why.

The effect of using different sampling techniques may be explored by repeating the experiment using a one-pound bag of individually wrapped fun size packs of "M&M's"® and giving each student a fun size pack for his or her individual sample. Ask the students the following questions:

- Are the ratios of the different colors in your fun size pack the same as the ratios you found in your individual sample in the original activity?
- In which individual sample are the ratios of the colors closest to the ratios found for the one-pound bag in the original activity? (These questions should be repeated for the group and class totals.)
- Are the ratios of the colors in the one-pound bag of fun size packs the same as the ratios you found in the one-pound bag of "M&M's"® in the original activity?

The *Exploring Data* and *Exploring Surveys and Information from Samples* books in the Quantitative Literacy Series published by Dale Seymour Publications also include a variety of interesting activities and problems to extend the concepts presented here.

IN THE CLASSROOM

This activity is appropriate for grades 5 through 8. Parts of it may also be used effectively with students in lower grade levels to introduce the various types of graphs. The first two pages of the activity may be done with any grade level. When used with primary students, the directions should be given orally. Students in grades 3 and 4 may do all the activity through problem 10 except for completing the Decimal Part and Percent columns in the tables and answering problem 7.

As noted, real graphs do not provide a practical method for displaying statistical data. However, it is important for elementary students to work with real graphs because they provide the connecting link between the physical data and their symbolic representation in a graph.

•Activity

STATISTICS WITH "M&M'S"®

"M&M's"® Plain Chocolate Candies come in six colors: brown, green, orange, red, tan, and yellow. *Before* you take a sample from the bag of "M&M's"®, answer the following questions:

1. Predict which color of "M&M's"® will occur most in the bag. _____
    In your sample. _____ Why did you predict these colors?

2. Predict which color of "M&M's"® will occur least in the bag. _____
    In your sample. _____ Why did you predict these colors?

Take a sample of "M&M's"® by dipping the measuring spoon into the bag of candy and removing a spoonful. *CAUTION, do not eat any of the "M&M's"®!*

Statistical data are often displayed graphically. Using a graph rather than simply presenting the data as a set of numbers makes it easier to study relationships in the data.

Arrange the "M&M's"® in your sample on Graph 1 on the next page. This type of graph is often called a *real graph* because the statistical data are displayed using the actual objects whose frequencies are being compared.

3. Record the total number of "M&M's"® and the number of each color of "M&M's"® in your sample.

    Total: _____ Brown: _____ Orange: _____ Tan: _____

    Green: _____ Red: _____ Yellow: _____

4. a. Which color occurs most often in your sample? _____

    b. Did you guess the color correctly in problem 1? _____

    c. Which color occurs least often in your sample? _____

    d. Did you guess the color correctly in problem 2? _____

As you remove each candy from the graph, shade in the circle it covered.

The type of graph you constructed is called a *pictograph* because the data are displayed using parallel columns (or rows) of pictures in which each picture represents one or more of the objects being compared.

CAUTION, do not eat any of the "M&M's"® yet!

Graph 1. Frequencies of "M&M's"®

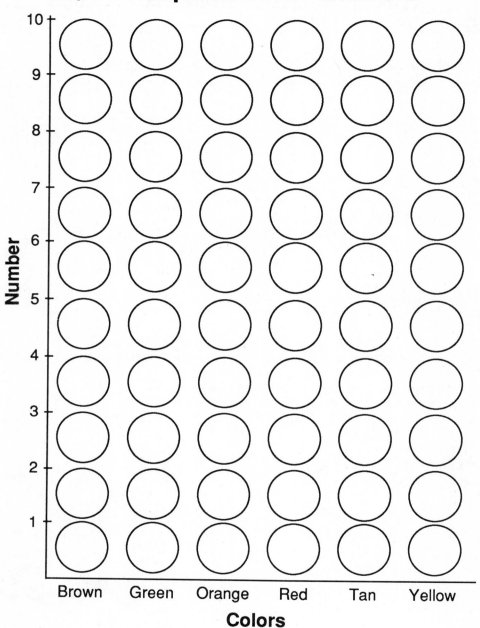

5. Compare your graph with the graphs of the other members of your group.

   a.   In what ways are the graphs alike?

   b.   How are they different?

6. On the basis of your sample, do you think you can accurately predict the number
   of each color of candy in a one-pound bag of "M&M's"® ? _____
   Why or why not?

Combine the data for your sample with the data for the other members of your group. Enter the group totals for each color of "M&M's"® in the Group Data table at the right.

Use the data to compare the number of each color with the total, and complete the Fractional Part, Decimal Part, and Percent columns in the table.

Group Data

Color	Number	Fractional Part	Decimal Part	Percent
Brown				
Green				
Orange				
Red				
Tan				
Yellow				
TOTAL				

7. Use the group totals to predict the number of each color of "M&M's"® you would expect to find in a one-pound bag of "M&M's"®.

Brown: _____   Orange: _____   Tan: _____

Green: _____   Red: _____   Yellow: _____

Describe the procedure you used to make your predictions.

Now you may eat the "M&M's"® in your sample.

8. What is your favorite color of "M&M's"® ? _____

Construct a bar graph for the group totals of each color of "M&M's"® in Graph 2. Label the divisions on the horizontal axis.

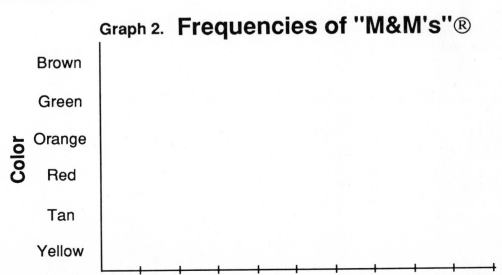

Graph 2. **Frequencies of "M&M's"®**

Thirteen charts have been put up at seven stations around your classroom. Go to each station, and use the data for your sample to make an entry on each chart that you find there.

On charts like the one at the right, mark an X in a square in the column that corresponds to the number of that color of "M&M's"® you found in your sample.

Charts like this one are examples of *line plots*. Line plots provide a quick, simple way to organize numerical data. They are constructed by drawing a horizontal number line (scale) and then marking an X above the appropriate coordinate for each data point. Line plots work best when there are fewer than 25 data points.

Red "M&M's"®

0	1	2	3	4	5	6	7	8	9	10	11	12	13	14	15

(X marked in column 6)

On charts like the one at the right, make a tally mark (|) in the square that corresponds to the number of that color of "M&M's"® you found in your sample.

On the Favorite Color chart, make a tally mark next to your favorite color of "M&M's"®.

Charts like these are examples of *frequency tables*. A frequency table shows how many times each data point occurs. They provide a quick method for tabulating data.

Red "M&M's"®			
Number in Sample	Tally	Frequency	Total
0			
1			
2			
3			
4			
5			
6				
7			
14			
15			
Total	✕		

9.   a. What general characteristics of a set of data can be obtained from a line plot?

   b. Can the same information be obtained from a frequency table?

Enter the class totals for each color of "M&M's"® in the table at the right. Use the data to complete the Fractional Part, Decimal Part, and Percent columns in the table.

Construct a pictograph for the number of each color of "M&M's"® on Graph 3 below. Hint: Let each circle represent more than one "M&M's"®.

Construct a bar graph for the number of each color of "M&M's"® on Graph 4, and label the divisions on the horizontal axis.

Class Data

Color	Number	Fractional Part	Decimal Part	Percent
Brown				
Green				
Orange				
Red				
Tan				
Yellow				
TOTAL				

Graph 3. **Frequencies of "M&M's"®**

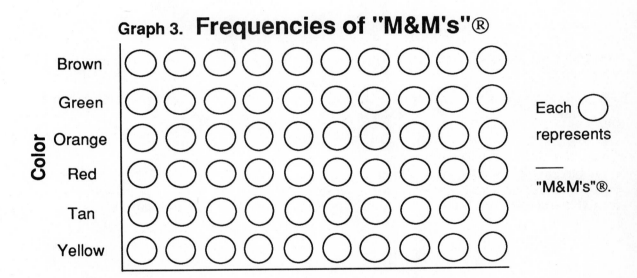

Graph 4. **Frequencies of "M&M's"®**

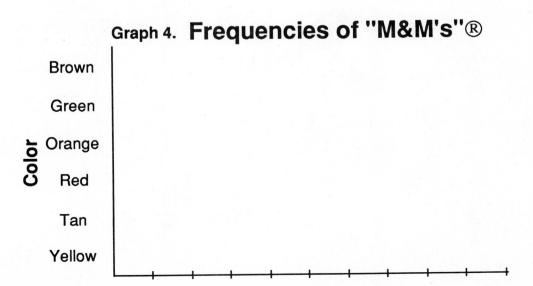

10. a. Which graph, the pictograph or the bar graph, was easier to construct? _____
     Why?

     b. Which graph is easier to read? _____ Why?

11. If you bought a one-pound bag of "M&M's"® Plain Chocolate Candies, how
     many of each color would you expect to find in it?

     Brown: _____   Orange: _____   Tan: _____

     Green: _____   Red: _____   Yellow: _____

     How do these totals compare with your answers to problem 7?

12. Help your classmates count the "M&M's"® remaining in the bag. What was the total
     number of each color of "M&M's"® in the bag?

     Brown: _____   Orange: _____   Tan: _____

     Green: _____   Red: _____   Yellow: _____

     How do these totals compare with the predictions you made in problem 11?

Use the class totals for favorite colors to complete the table
at the right.

13. If you were the manufacturer of "M&M's"®, how might
     you use the data in the Favorite Color table?

FAVORITE COLOR		
Color	Number	Percent
Brown		
Green		
Orange		
Red		
Tan		
Yellow		
Total		

TABLES FOR "M&M'S"®

_____ "M&M's"®

0	1	2	3	4	5	6	7	8	9	10	11	12	13	14	15

"M&M's"® _____

Number in Sample	Tally	Frequency	Total
0			
1			
2			
3			
4			
5			
6			
7			
8			
9			
10			
11			
12			
13			
14			
15			
Total			

FAVORITE COLOR

Color	Tally	Frequency
Brown		
Green		
Orange		
Red		
Tan		
Yellow		
Total		

III. THE WEATHER REPORT

PURPOSE   This activity applies many concepts of data analysis, including reading and interpreting data, constructing stem-and-leaf plots, box-and-whisker plots, and line graphs, determining the range of data and measures of central tendency, and evaluating statements based on data. In the activity, students analyze the advantages and disadvantages of using different displays of data.

MATERIALS   For each student:

- a calculator
- graph paper

REQUIRED BACKGROUND   Students should know:

- the concepts of mean, median, and mode and be able to determine each
- how to construct the various displays of data described in the Purpose section

TIME REQUIREMENT   40 to 50 minutes

GETTING STARTED   This activity should follow classroom instruction on the various concepts contained in the activity. It would be helpful if students first completed the What's the Average? activity, as it develops the concepts of mean and median and explores the effects of extremes in data. This activity will extend and reinforce the concepts explored in What's the Average?.

KEY IDEAS   The focus of the activity is to analyze the various plots, to determine what information can be more easily derived from one display than another, and to evaluate the use of mean or median as a good descriptor of average.

Advertisers, policy makers, and decision makers constantly use the term *average,* but the average reported may not accurately describe the entire set of data. It is very important to know the range of data to fully understand what the mean or median really indicates.

For example, the mean temperatures for San Francisco and Wichita differ by only a degree. The same is true for the median temperatures; however, the range of the data varies considerably. There are only two months when the temperature for Wichita even falls within the annual temperature range of San Francisco.

The stem-and-leaf plots illustrate the difference in range of data, but the difference is much more visually apparent when depicted in line graphs or in the side by side box-and-whisker plots. One can identify the median and the upper and lower quartiles of data in the stem-and-leaf plot; however, the relationships among all these measures are much clearer in the box-and-whisker plots. Each display has its own unique characteristics, and each offers a different insight into the data. These similarities and differences should be analyzed and evaluated in class discussion. Questions for the class might include the following:

- What are the advantages and disadvantages of stem-and-leaf and box-and-whisker plots?

- What information is contained in a stem-and-leaf plot that is not in a box-and-whisker plot, and vice versa?
- What information can you derive from a line graph that you cannot find in the stem-and-leaf or box-and-whisker plot?
- Describe a problem situation for which you would use each display of data, and explain why you would choose that particular means rather than another for that situation.

EXTENSIONS   One average that interests all students is the "class average" or "test average." This activity can be extended to explore "average grades." The numerical values of the temperatures for San Francisco and Wichita in the first part of the activity could easily be considered as the mean scores on weekly tests for two classes. Students may then investigate questions such as:

- How well does the average score describe the results in each class?
- Which class had the better overall results? Why, since the averages were about the same?
- Remove the two lowest or two highest grades in each class. What effect does this have on the class average?
- Is the net effect of removing these scores the same in each class? Why?

Students can also analyze how a change in the vertical scale on a graph changes the visual impact of the data. The stem-and-leaf plot, box-and-whisker plot, and the graph of the weather data for San Francisco all display very consistent data with a small range, whereas the range of data for Wichita is large in each display.

Construct a new graph of the data for Wichita. Use the same horizontal scale for the months, but change the vertical scale so that each interval between lines represents 20 degrees. Now compare the visual impact of this new graph with the graph of the San Francisco data.

- How has the change in the vertical scale changed the image of the data?
- Does this graph illustrate data that appear to be about the same as the data for San Francisco?
- As a member of the Wichita Chamber of Commerce, would you use this graph or the first one constructed to advertise the climate in your city?

Have students describe real situations in which two parties debating an issue might display the same data using two different vertical scales to prove their point (for example, a salesperson and a company manager discussing previous years' sales data during negotiation for a salary increase). Have students develop a set of data, construct two different graphs, and present two opposing and convincing arguments on the issue.

Exploring Data in the Quantatative Literacy Series, published by Dale Seymour Publications, includes a variety of interesting activities and problems to extend the concepts presented here. *Data Insights,* a computer software program from Sunburst Communications, can be used to construct stem-and-leaf plots, box-and-whisker plots, and line graphs.

IN THE CLASSROOM   This activity can be used in grades 6 through 8 after the students are familiar with the concepts of mean, median, and mode and the construction of the various displays of data. Students at this age may not understand the full significance of the uses of averages as applied in the real world. They should explore the various problems in the activity and the Extensions section to develop their understanding that the use of the word *average* can be deceiving.

The eight cities in the table in the activity were chosen because they provide interesting examples of the similarities and differences in climate between pairs of cities. Some pairs with approximately the same annual mean or median temperature but with sharply contrasting climates lie on the same latitude. One pair is in the same state, only 280 miles apart. A city that is farther north (Seattle) has a more temperate climate than another city to the south (Portland, OR). All cities except San Francisco and Los Angeles have maximum temperatures in July and August. Discussions involving the latitude and geographical locations of the cities and the effects of the jet streams, ocean currents, and geological formations provide meaningful problem situations in which mathematics can be connected to other subjects, such as social studies, geography, and science.

• Activity

THE WEATHER REPORT

Normal Daily Temperature for Some U.S. Cities
Based on the Period from 1950 to 1980

	Jan	Feb	Mar	Apr	May	Jun	Jul	Aug	Sep	Oct	Nov	Dec
Los Angeles, CA	56	57	57	60	62	66	69	70	70	66	61	57
San Francisco, CA	49	52	53	55	58	61	62	63	64	61	55	49
Wichita, KS	30	35	44	56	66	76	81	80	71	59	44	34
Portland, ME	22	23	32	43	53	62	68	67	59	48	38	26
Portland, OR	39	43	46	50	57	63	68	67	63	54	46	41
Charlotte, NC	41	43	50	60	68	75	79	78	72	61	51	43
Seattle, WA	39	43	44	49	55	60	65	64	60	53	45	41
Spokane, WA	26	32	38	46	54	62	70	69	59	48	35	29

SOURCE: U.S. National Oceanic and Atmospheric Administration

1. Construct a stem-and-leaf plot for the weather data given for San Francisco and Wichita.

SAN FRANCISCO

```
6 |
5 |
4 |
```

WICHITA

```
8 |
7 |
6 |
5 |
4 |
3 |
2 |
```

2. Compute the mean, median, and mode for the data given for San Francisco and Wichita.

Temperature Averages		
	San Francisco	**Wichita**
Mean		
Median		
Mode		

3. Construct a line graph for the temperatures for San Francisco and Wichita on the grid below.

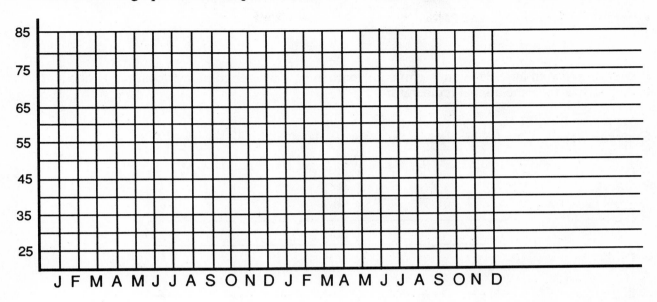

4. Using the scale on the grid above, construct a vertical box-and-whisker plot for the temperatures for San Francisco and Wichita to the right of the line graphs.

5. Draw a horizontal line through the graphs to show the median for each set of data.

6. For how many months of the year is the temperature in Wichita within the range of the temperatures in San Francisco? _____

7. Which display of data can be most easily used to answer problem 6? _____
   Explain why or why not for each display.

8. The Wichita Chamber of Commerce could advertise that "the annual average temperature in Wichita is the same as that in *balmy* San Francisco." Evaluate this claim on the basis of the actual temperature data.

9. The annual mean and median temperatures for these two cities are nearly the same. Compare how accurately the means and the medians describe the climate in each city.

10. What other information do you need in addition to the median or mean to accurately describe the annual temperatures?

11. Find the latitude of Wichita and San Francisco.

    a. San Francisco _____   b. Wichita _____

    c. Which city is farther north? _____

12. If the difference in latitude is not significant, explain how the geographical location of each city affects the annual temperature.

13. Construct a back to back stem-and-leaf plot for Portland, ME, and Portland, OR.

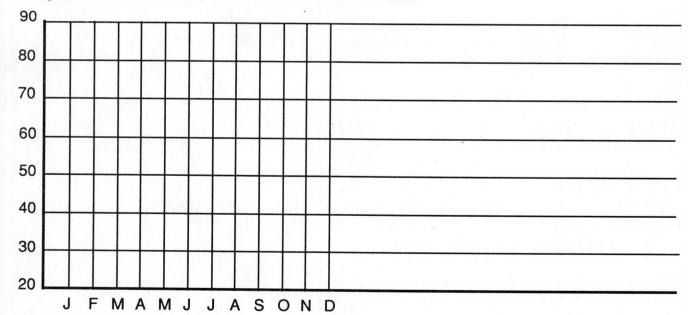

PORTLAND, ME   **PORTLAND, OR**

	8	
	7	
	6	
	5	
	4	
	3	
	2	

14. On the grid below, construct line graphs and accompanying vertical box-and-whisker plots for the weather data for the two cities; then draw the median lines. Explore problems similar to 7, 8, and 10 for these two sets of data.

15. Choose other pairs of cities from the table on page 132, and construct various displays for the data on graph paper. Explore similarities and differences in the data. Determine the latitude and geographical location of each city. Explain how these affect similarities or differences in the climates of the chosen cities.

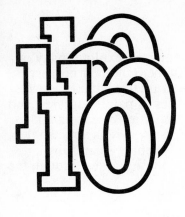

INTRODUCTION TO GEOMETRY

ACTIVITIES:
I. CLASSIFYING TRIANGLES AND QUADRILATERALS
II. TRIANGLE PROPERTIES

I. CLASSIFYING TRIANGLES AND QUADRILATERALS

PURPOSE This activity reinforces classification of triangles and quadrilaterals according to the side and angle relationships of the figures.

MATERIALS For each two or three students:

- a centimeter ruler
- a protractor
- scissors
- copies of the Triangles page (p. 141) and Quadrilaterals page (p. 142)

REQUIRED BACKGROUND Students should know:

- the geometry vocabulary used in the activity
- how to measure angles and line segments

TIME REQUIREMENT
- Classifying Triangles: 20 to 25 minutes
- Classifying Quadrilaterals: 20 to 25 minutes

GETTING STARTED Students should work together in groups to share information on the necessary measurements and to discuss the sorting of the polygons into various groupings. However, each student should complete the problems on the activity pages alone. Students should be reminded that measurement is not exact, and thus the sum of the measures of the angles in the triangles and quadrilaterals may not result in the exact theoretical total. Precise understanding of the definitions of the special quadrilaterals is not necessary, as the definitions will be reinforced in the activity

KEY IDEAS In the Classifiying Triangles activity, students will find that classifying triangles using both sides and angles gives a more precise description of the triangle than classifying by sides or angles only. Problem 9 can be used to review the indirect method of reasoning.

In the Classifying Quadrilaterals activity, students will explore many of the properties of special quadrilaterals and classify them by their properties. In problems 13 through 18, some students may not initially include squares as rectangles or parallelograms or include rhombuses as parallelograms, and so forth. Students should quickly realize that all properties of a rectangle or rhombus are also properties of a square, and thus a square is a rectangle and also a rhombus. Teachers should review these problems carefully since students will better understand the classification of these figures through the analysis of these properties.

Answers to problems 25 through 29 may vary considerably for different students, and careful attention should be paid to students' responses. The answers may provide the clearest insight into students' understanding of the special quadrilaterals and their respective properties. If a student objects to a definition, then he or she should provide the counterexample to illustrate why a definition is not accurate.

These activities can be related to the Attributes and What's Different? activities in Chapter 2. In those activities, geometric figures of various sizes, shapes, and shading were sorted on the basis of these attributes. In these activities, we extend the process and vocabulary. The shapes are now precisely defined, and the attributes are the properties of the figures. Whereas in Chapter 2, one difference for the attribute pieces might be shading or size, here one difference between a square and a rhombus is the presence of a right angle. This one difference results in a new shape with a new name.

At the end of these activities, students should be able to construct a chart of quadrilaterals and illustrate the hierarchy of the figures and the relationships among them. For each pair of quadrilaterals joined by a segment (such as parallelogram and rectangle), students should be able to specify the difference between the two figures. They should also be able to define any quadrilateral as a member of some other set but with additional properties. Relating one figure to the other sets to which it belongs and stating which additional properties are needed to define it will deepen students' understanding of the various quadrilaterals and the relationships among them.

EXTENSIONS   The study of quadrilaterals and the understanding of their properties can be extended by using the Mysterious Midpoints activity in Chapter 14. Students should also be encouraged to read material on the Van Hiele levels that describes the development of mental processes as related to the understanding of geometry. Class discussion might focus on how the questions and problems in this activity help elementary school students to progress through the various levels. Some questions that might be posed to students include:

• Which problems or questions in the Classifying Triangles activity are at level 0, 1, or 2?
• Classify the sets of problems in the Classifying Quadrilaterals activity according to the Van Hiele levels.
• What other questions might be asked to determine the level of students' understanding of the classification of triangles and quadrilaterals?
• At what level would you place a middle grade student who could successfully complete this activity?

IN THE CLASSROOM   This activity is appropriate for grades 5 through 8. Various problems may be used whenever those specific topics are being presented. The questions and problems should be adapted to fit the material being covered and the level of students' understanding. These activities will help middle school students progress from one Van Hiele level to another and thus will greatly enhance their understanding of geometry.

● Activity

CLASSIFYING TRIANGLES

For each triangle on the Triangles page (p. 141), find the measure of each angle and the length of each side. Indicate the measures inside each figure, then cut out each triangle.

Triangles may be classified in two ways:

A. By the number of congruent sides:
   1.   A *scalene* triangle has no congruent sides.
   2.   An *isosceles* triangle has at least two congruent sides.
   3.   An *equilateral* triangle has three congruent sides.

B. By the types of angles:
   1.   An *acute* triangle has three acute angles.
   2.   A *right* triangle has a right angle.
   3.   An *obtuse* triangle has an obtuse angle.

Sort the triangles using the definitions above. In the blanks below, write the letter of each triangle that belongs in each group. A triangle may belong to more than one group.

1. Scalene _____   2. Acute _____

3. Right _____   4. Equilateral _____

5. Isosceles _____   6. Obtuse _____

7.   Is it possible to sort all the triangles using:

   a.   two classifications by sides (such as isosceles and scalene) ? _____
        Explain.

   b.   two classifications by angles (such as right and obtuse)? _____
        Explain.

8.   List all the possible ways to sort triangles using only two classifications, one by side and one by angle. Sort the triangles according to your groups of two classifications, and indicate the letters of the triangles that belong in each category.

9.   Are there any combinations of two classifications, one by side and one by angle, that are not possible?   If so, which one(s) and why?

• Activity

CLASSIFYING QUADRILATERALS

For each figure on the Quadrilaterals page (p. 142), find the measure of each angle and the length of each side. Indicate the measures inside each figure, then carefully cut out each quadrilateral. Sort the quadrilaterals into groups according to the following properties. Figures may be placed into more than one group. Indicate the letters of the quadrilaterals that have each property.

1. All sides are congruent   _____

2. Exactly one pair of parallel sides   _____

3. More than one right angle   _____

4. Diagonals are congruent   _____

5. Two pairs of opposite sides are parallel   _____

6. Diagonals bisect each other   _____

7. Two pairs of opposite sides are congruent   _____

8. Diagonals are perpendicular   _____

9. Two pairs of opposite angles are congruent   _____

10. Has one or more lines of symmetry   _____

11. Has rotational symmetry
    (turn must be less than 360°)   _____

12. Adjacent sides are congruent   _____

Identify the letters of the figures that are:

13. Squares   _____   14. Rectangles   _____

15. Parallelograms   _____   16. Trapezoids   _____

17. Rhombuses   _____   18. Kites   _____

Which of the properties named in problems 1 through 12 above does each of the following quadrilaterals have? Write the correct numbers in the blanks below.

19. Rectangle   _____   20. Square   _____

21. Parallelogram   _____   22. Rhombus   _____

23. Trapezoid   _____   24. Kite   _____

On the basis of your answers to problems 19 through 24, write a definition for *square, parallelogram, rectangle, trapezoid, and rhombus*. Use the least number of properties possible to define each polygon.

25. A *square* is a quadrilateral with

26. A *parallelogram* is a quadrilateral with

27. A *rectangle* is a quadrilateral with

28. A *trapezoid* is a quadrilateral with

29. A *rhombus* is a quadrilateral with

30. In problems 25 through 29, let SQ, PR, RC, TR, and RH, respectively, designate the sets of quadrilaterals you defined. Which sets are subsets of another set?

31. Construct a tree diagram showing the relationships among the following quadrilaterals: trapezoid, parallelogram, rectangle, rhombus, kite, and square. Start with Quadrilateral at the top, as shown below. As you proceed down, each line segment connecting two figures will indicate that the figures below are subsets of the figures above.

QUADRILATERAL

TRIANGLES

QUADRILATERALS

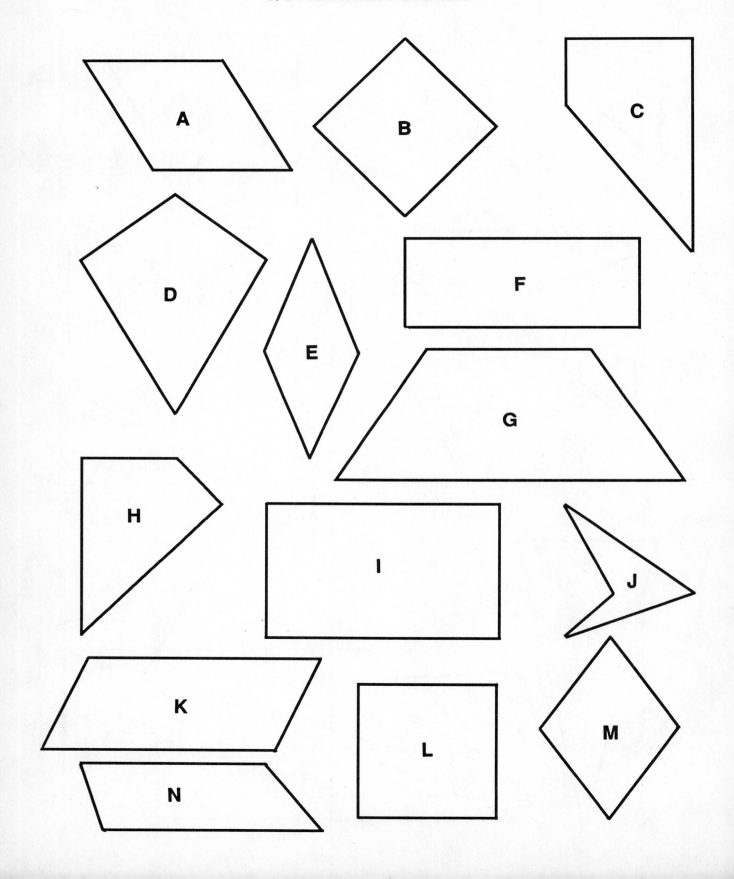

II. TRIANGLE PROPERTIES

PURPOSE
These activities informally develop the theorems on the angle sum of a triangle and the triangle inequality. These activities also introduce the concepts of similarity and congruence and the conditions necessary for two triangles to be congruent.

MATERIALS
For each student:

- a centimeter ruler
- a compass
- a protractor
- a calculator

REQUIRED BACKGROUND
Students should:

- know how to duplicate a line segment and an angle using a straightedge and a compass
- know how to measure and draw an angle using a protractor
- be familiar with the concept of a ratio
- be able to classify triangles by the number of congruent sides and the types of angles

TIME REQUIREMENT
- Triangle Properties: 50 to 60 minutes
- To Be or Not To Be Congruent?: 50 to 60 minutes

GETTING STARTED
Triangle Properties and To Be or Not To Be Congruent? are independent activities. Students may do To Be or Not To Be Congruent? without doing Triangle Properties first.

Students should work in groups of two or three when completing the activities. Doing so enhances the activity by allowing students to discuss the results as they obtain them, and it reduces the amount of time required by allowing the students to share the task of construction. It may also be beneficial for students to complete the Classifying Triangles and Classifying Quadrilaterals activities before doing this activity.

All the constructions should be done on a separate sheet of paper and numbered. Emphasize that, to obtain accurate results, students must construct the figures carefully.

KEY IDEAS
TRIANGLE PROPERTIES Problems 3 through 13 develop the triangle inequality, which states that the sum of the lengths of any two sides of a triangle is greater than the length of the third side. If the construction in problem 8 is not done accurately, students may erroneously conclude that the correct statement of the theorem is that the sum of the lengths of any two sides must be greater than *or equal to* the length of the third side. Examine the constructions in problems 6 through 8 carefully to clarify how the situation changes as the sum of the lengths of two sides is less than, equal to, and greater than the length of the third side.

Problems 15 through 24 develop the theorem that the sum of the measures of the angles of a triangle is always 180°. Because a protractor is an inaccurate measuring device, the sum of the measures of the angles obtained by students may differ slightly from 180°. The fact that the discrepancy is due to errors in measurement can be illustrated by having students cut out one of the triangles they constructed and then tear off two of the angles and rearrange them at the third vertex to form a line segment, as illustrated below.

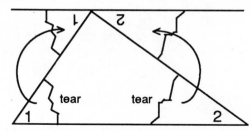

Problem 25 develops the concept of similar triangles. As the problem illustrates, two triangles are similar if two angles of one triangle are congruent to two angles of the other. The importance of similar triangles lies in the fact that, if two triangles are similar, then the ratios of their corresponding sides are constant. This fact is derived in problem 25c.

TO BE OR NOT TO BE CONGRUENT? This activity develops the concept of congruent triangles and explores the conditions necessary to ensure that two triangles are congruent, that is, that their corresponding sides and angles have the same measures. The following list relates the key concepts to the corresponding activities:

Two triangles are congruent if:

- the lengths of the sides of one triangle are equal to the lengths of the sides of the other. (Problems 3 through 8 and 14b of Triangle Properties)
- two sides and the included angle of one triangle are congruent to two sides and the included angle of the other. (Problems 1 through 4 of To Be or Not To Be Congruent?)
- two angles and the included side of one triangle are congruent to two angles and the included side of the other. (Problems 5 through 8 of To Be or Not To Be Congruent?)

Since the sum of the measures of the angles of a triangle is always 180°, if two angles of one triangle are congruent to two angles of the other, then the third angles are also congruent. It follows from the third theorem above that, if two angles and the side opposite one of them in a triangle are congruent to the corresponding parts in another triangle, then the two triangles are congruent. This result is investigated in problem 9.

Problems 10 through 13 explore the ambiguous case where two sides and the angle opposite one of the sides in one triangle are congruent to the corresponding parts in another triangle. In this situation, there are two possibilities: the triangles are distinct, or they are congruent right triangles.

EXTENSIONS   The activities may be extended by using the angle sum of a triangle to derive a formula for the angle sum of an *n*-gon. One can also investigate how the lengths of four segments must be related in order to determine the sides of a quadrilateral. The teacher should also extend the concepts of similarity and congruence to other polygons.

IN THE CLASSROOM   These activities may be used in grades 6 through 10. They provide the prerequisite concrete experiences with many of the fundamental geometric concepts that are formalized in a high school geometry course.

·Activity

TRIANGLE PROPERTIES

Use a ruler to construct two different triangles in which one side is 4 cm and another side is 6 cm.

1. Compare your triangles with a classmate's. What do you notice?

2. How many different triangles could you construct given the length of two sides?

In problems 3 through 8, use a ruler and a compass to construct a triangle with sides of the specified lengths.

3. 12 cm, 10 cm, 8 cm   4. 12 cm, 12 cm, 8 cm   5. 10 cm, 10 cm, 10 cm

6. 6 cm, 5 cm, 12 cm   7. 7 cm, 5 cm, 11 cm   8. 10 cm, 6 cm, 4 cm

9. a. Which of problems 3 through 8 *did not* result in a triangle?

    b. In these cases, what is true about the sum of the lengths of the two shorter sides?

10. a. Which of problems 3 through 8 *did* result in a triangle?

    b. In these cases, what is true about the sum of the lengths of the two shorter sides?

11. List three sets of three lengths that *can* be used to construct a triangle. Do not use more than one set in which all the lengths are equal.

    a. _____   b. _____   c. _____

12. List three sets of three lengths that *cannot* be used to construct a triangle.

    a. _____   b. _____   c. _____

13. What can you conclude about the lengths of the sides of a triangle?

14. For each of problems 3 through 8 that resulted in a triangle:

    a. Identify the type of triangle that was constructed.

    b. Compare the triangle with a classmate's. What do you notice?

In problems 15 through 20, use a ruler and a protractor to construct a triangle that has two angles with the indicated measures. Record your results in the table.

15. 30°, 50°   16. 40°, 50°   17. 90°, 95°

18. 60°, 60°   19. 110°, 70°   20. 80°, 80°

Problem	Sum of the Given Angles	Is a Triangle Possible?	If Yes, What Is the Measure of the Third Angle?
15			
16			
17			
18			
19			
20			

21. a. In each of problems 15 through 20 that *did not* result in a triangle, what is true about the sum of the measures of the two given angles?

    b. In each of problems 15 through 20 that *did* result in a triangle, what is true about the sum of the measures of the two given angles?

22. List three pairs of angles that *can* be used to construct a triangle.

    a. _____   b. _____   c. _____

23. List three pairs of angles that *cannot* be used to construct a triangle.

    a. _____   b. _____   c. _____

24. What can you conclude about the sum of the measures of the angles of a triangle?

25. For each of problems 15 through 20 that resulted in a triangle:

    a. Identify the type of triangle that was constructed.

    b. Compare the triangle with a classmate's. What do you notice?

    c. Measure the lengths of the sides of each of your triangles in problems 15
       through 20. Then find the ratio of the length of each side of your triangle to
       the length of the corresponding side of your classmate's triangle, and record
       the ratios for each triangle in the table below.

| Problem | Ratios of Lengths of Sides | | | | | |
| | Shortest Side to Shortest Side | | Middle Side to Middle Side | | Longest Side to Longest Side | |
	Fraction	Decimal	Fraction	Decimal	Fraction	Decimal

    d. For each pair of triangles, what can you conclude about the ratios of the
       corresponding sides?

•Activity
_____

TO BE OR NOT TO BE CONGRUENT?

Two triangles are *congruent* if the measures of their corresponding sides and angles are equal. In Triangle Properties, you learned that, if the lengths of the sides of one triangle are equal to the lengths of the sides of another triangle, then the two triangles must be congruent. That is, the measures of the corresponding angles of the triangles must also be equal. You also discovered that the converse is not true. It is possible to have two triangles in which the measures of the angles are equal but the measures of the corresponding sides are not equal.

This activity investigates the question, "Are there combinations of three corresponding congruent parts of two triangles, other than the sides, that will ensure that the triangles are congruent?"

In problems 1 through 3, use a ruler and a compass to construct a triangle with the given parts.

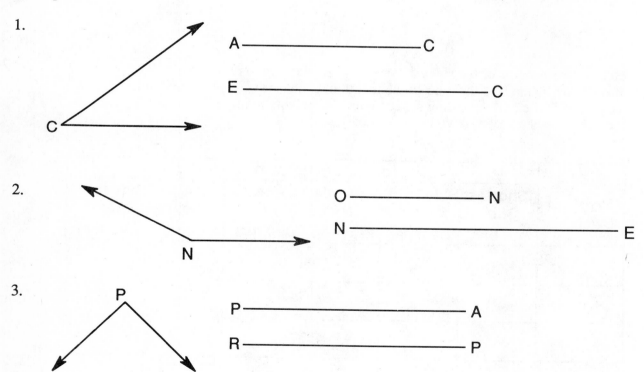

1.

A————————C

E——————————————C

C (angle)

2.

N (angle)

O————————N

N————————————————————E

3.

P (angle)

P————————————A

R————————————P

4.   a. In problems 1 through 3, how are the given sides and angle of the triangle related?

   b. Compare the triangles you constructed in problems 1 through 3 with those of a classmate. What do you notice?

   c. What can you conclude from parts a and b?

In problems 5 through 7, use a ruler and a compass to construct a triangle with the given parts.

5.

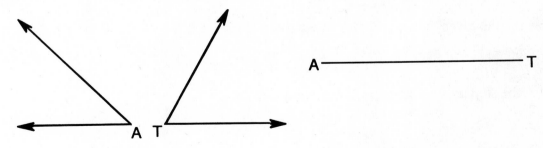

6.

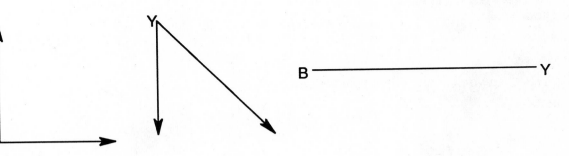

7.

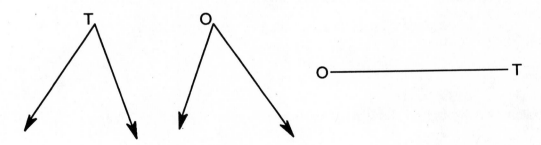

8. a. In problems 5 through 7, how are the given side and angles of the triangle related?

b. Compare the triangles you constructed in problems 5 through 7 with those of a classmate. What do you notice?

c. What can you conclude from parts a and b?

9. Use a ruler and a protractor to construct a triangle BAD in which AB = 6 cm, m ∠ A = 40°, and m ∠ D = 80°.

   a. How are the given side and angles of the triangle related?

   b. Describe step by step how you constructed the triangle.

   c. Compare the triangle you constructed with that of a classmate. What do you notice?

   d. What can you conclude from parts a and c?

In problems 10 through 12, use a ruler, a protractor, and a compass to construct a triangle with the given parts.

10. TO = 5 cm
    OP = 3 cm
    m ∠ T = 30°

11. HA = 10 cm
    AT = 6 cm
    m ∠ H = 37°

12. TI = 9 cm
    IE = 4 cm
    m ∠ T = 40°

13. a. In problems 10 through 12, how are the given sides and angle of the triangle related?

    b. Which of problems 10 through 12 did not result in a triangle?

    c. Did any of the problems result in more than one triangle?

    d. If any problem resulted in only one triangle, what type of triangle was it?

    e. What can you conclude from parts a through d?

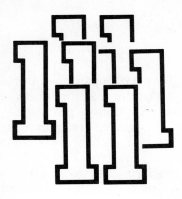

CONGRUENCE AND SIMILARITY

ACTIVITIES:
I.   ART AND GEOMETRY
II. OUTDOOR GEOMETRY

I. ART AND GEOMETRY

PURPOSE   This activity explores the application of similarity in drawing objects in three-dimensional perspective. The concept of a dilation, or a similarity transformation, is developed, and the relationship between the areas of similar figures is explored.

MATERIALS   For each student:

- a centimeter ruler
- a protractor

REQUIRED BACKGROUND   Students should:

- understand the concepts of similarity and congruence
- know how to measure segments and angles
- be able to determine ratios of the lengths of corresponding sides of similar polygons

TIME REQUIREMENT
- A Problem of Perspective: 50 to 60 minutes
- Dilations: 50 to 60 minutes

GETTING STARTED   These two activities are independent. Students may complete Dilations without first completing A Problem of Perspective. Students may work independently or in small groups. No prior instruction is needed.

KEY IDEAS   **A PROBLEM OF PERSPECTIVE** Perspective is a fundamental concept in art. Two sets of points are in perspective if the lines drawn through corresponding points of the two sets are concurrent. The point where the lines intersect is called the *vanishing point*. This concept is illustrated in the activity by drawing lines through the vertices of the pyramids PYRA and MIDS. It may also be used to show that the pyramids MIDS and CONE are not in perspective since the lines drawn through the vertices of these pyramids are parallel. When objects that are not in perspective (such as the pyramids MIDS and CONE) are portrayed against objects that are in perspective (the checkerboard), an *illusion* of perspective is created.

If an entire drawing is in perspective, the vanishing points for the perspective lines for different sets of points must all be collinear. The line containing the vanishing points is called the *axis of perspective* or the *horizon line*. This concept is explored in problem 4.

In problem 4, students should recognize that the two objects drawn in perspective are scale drawings of one another and that the scale factor is the ratio of the distances from the vanishing point to corresponding points on the objects. The transformations used to achieve perspective are examples of *similarity transformations*.

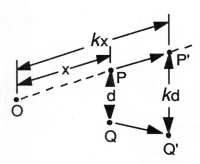

DILATIONS This activity explores the idea of a similarity transformation, or dilation, and illustrates how a dilation may be used to enlarge or reduce a figure. Similarity transformations are defined by a point, sometimes referred to as the *similarity point,* and a *scale factor.* In the drawing at the left, if O is the similarity point and k is the scale factor, then the image, P', of a point P is a point on the ray OP, and the distance from O to P' is k times the distance from O to P. In addition, the distance between the images of any two points is k times the distance between the original points. If $k > 1$, then all points are moved away from O, and the figure is enlarged; if $k < 1$, all points are moved toward O, and the figure is reduced. In this sense, a dilation may be thought of as either a stretching or a shrinking of the plane defined by the point O and the scale factor k.

It is important for students to understand that, in this activity, they are working with three similarity transformations, not just one. The first has similarity point P and scale factor 2:1, the second has similarity point P and scale factor 3:1, and the third has similarity point Q and scale factor 2:1.

Students should also recognize that a dilation does not preserve the distance between points, but it does preserve collinearity, betweenness of points, and the measure of angles. They should also realize that a figure and its image are always similar and that, if the scale factor is k, then the area of the image is k^2 times the area of the original figure.

EXTENSIONS

These activities should be extended by having students investigate other properties of dilations. For example:

- Given $\triangle ABC$ and similarity point P, how would you locate points A', B', and C' so that the scale factor is 1:2?
- Are the images of parallel lines always parallel?
- For each dilation in the activity, not only were the triangle and its image similar, but they were also similarly situated; that is, their corresponding sides were parallel. Will this always be true?
- Given any two similar triangles, is it possible to define a similarity transformation that will map one of the triangles onto the other?
- How would the dilation in problem 1 change if point A' is marked so that P is between A and A' and PA' = 2 x PA, B' is marked so that P is between B and B' and PB' = 2 x PB, and C' is marked so that P is between C and C' and PC' = 2 x PC?

Students should also examine pictures of major art works and drawings from newspapers and magazines and identify examples of vanishing points, horizon lines, and dilations. They may also find it interesting to investigate other optical illusions created through improper use of perspective.

Students should be encouraged to explore the artwork of M. C. Escher, who used similarity relations extensively to create illusions in his works. Several books on Escher's works are available from various publishers.

IN THE CLASSROOM

These activities are appropriate for grades 7 to 10 to extend the concept of similarity and to illustrate its practical uses.

•Activity

A PROBLEM OF PERSPECTIVE

1. a. Which pyramid in the drawing below appears to be the largest? ____________

   b. Which appears to be the smallest? ____________

   c. Measure the lengths of segments $\overline{YA}$, $\overline{IS}$, and $\overline{OE}$.

   YA = ________ IS = ________ OE = ________

   d. Were you surprised by the length of any of the segments in part c?

   e. Express each of the following ratios as a decimal rounded to the nearest hundredth.

   YA:IS ________ YA:OE ________ IS:OE ________

Figure 1

The optical illusion in Figure 1, which makes pyramid CONE appear to be smaller than pyramid MIDS, is known as an *illusion of perspective*. Making objects appear to be at different depths and in the correct proportions to one another is very important in art. Artists such as Leonardo da Vinci studied perspective during the Renaissance and developed its principles using simple geometric concepts. The artist represents a three-dimensional scene, such as pyramids on a checkerboard, by using two-dimensional figures in a particular ratio of scale. The eye interprets these two-dimensional figures drawn on a flat surface as three-dimensional objects in perspective in space. The *illusion* of perspective is created when forms that are not in perspective are drawn over forms that are in perspective (in this case, the checkerboard).

2.   Measure angles and segments in Figure 1 as necessary to answer the following questions.

   a.   How are quadrilaterals PYRA and MIDS related?   _____
        Explain.

   b.   How are quadrilaterals PYRA and CONE related?   _____
        Explain.

   c.   How are quadrilaterals CONE and MIDS related?   _____
        Explain.

3.   In Figure 1, draw lines $\overleftrightarrow{YI}$, $\overleftrightarrow{PM}$, and $\overleftrightarrow{AS}$, and label the point where they intersect, V_1. Express each of the following ratios as a decimal rounded to the nearest hundredth:

   a. $YV_1 : IV_1$ _____

   b. $PV_1 : MV_1$ _____

   c. $AV_1 : SV_1$ _____

   d.   How do these ratios compare with the ratio $YA : IS$ in problem 1?

4. In Figure 1, draw lines $\overleftrightarrow{ZL}$, $\overleftrightarrow{XQ}$, $\overleftrightarrow{WT}$, and $\overleftrightarrow{VU}$, and label the point where they intersect, V_2. Draw line $\overleftrightarrow{V_1V_2}$.

   a. How do lines $\overleftrightarrow{V_1V_2}$, $\overleftrightarrow{LU}$, and $\overleftrightarrow{ZV}$ appear to be related?

   b. Artists refer to line $\overleftrightarrow{V_1V_2}$ as the *horizon line*. Why do you think they chose this term?

   c. Artists refer to points V_1 and V_2 as *vanishing points*. Why do you think they chose this term?

   d. Mathematicians refer to points V_1 and V_2 as *similarity points*. Why is this term appropriate?

5. Draw lines $\overleftrightarrow{YO}$, $\overleftrightarrow{RN}$, and $\overleftrightarrow{AE}$, and label the point where they intersect, V_3. Express each of the following ratios as a decimal rounded to the nearest hundredth:

   a. $YV_3 : OV_3$ _____

   b. $RV_3 : NV_3$ _____

   c. $AV_3 : EV_3$ _____

   d. How do these ratios compare with the ratio YA:OE in problem 1?

   e. Mathematicians refer to these ratios as *scale factors*. Why is this term appropriate?

• Looking Back

DILATIONS

The transformations that artists use to solve the problem of perspective are called *dilations* or *similarity transformations*. In this activity, we will explore the properties of dilations.

In Figure 2 below:

A. Draw rays $\overrightarrow{PA}$, $\overrightarrow{PB}$, and $\overrightarrow{PC}$.

B. Mark point A' on $\overrightarrow{PA}$, such that A is between P and A' and PA = AA'.

C. Mark point B' on $\overrightarrow{PB}$, such that B is between P and B' and PB = BB'.

D. Mark point C' on $\overrightarrow{PC}$, such that C is between P and C' and PC = CC'.

E. Draw ΔA'B'C'.

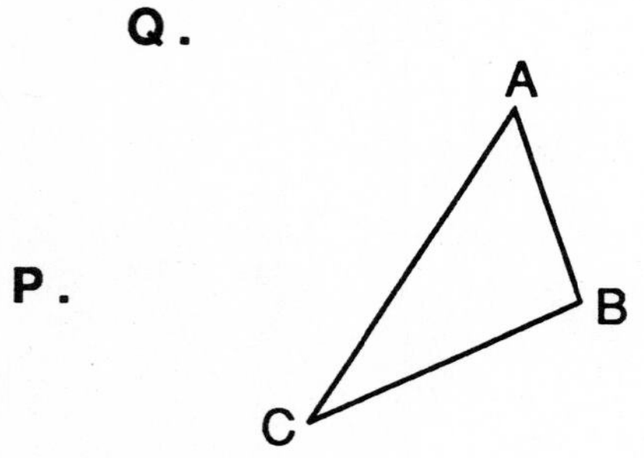

Q .

P .

Figure 2

6. a. Is ΔABC similar to ΔA'B'C'? _____ Explain.

b. What is the scale factor? _____

c. What is the ratio of PA' to PA? _____

7.   Find the midpoints of segments $\overline{A'B'}$, $\overline{B'C'}$, and $\overline{C'A'}$, and label them R, S, and T, respectively. Draw $\triangle RST$.

   a.   Drawing $\triangle RST$ divided $\triangle A'B'C'$ into four triangles. What is the relationship among the triangles?

   b.   How is $\triangle STR$ related to $\triangle ABC$?

   c.   How is the area of $\triangle A'B'C'$ related to the area of $\triangle ABC$?

In Figure 2:

A.   Mark point A" on $\overrightarrow{PA}$, such that A is between P and A" and AA" = 2 x PA.
B.   Mark point B" on $\overrightarrow{PB}$, such that B is between P and B" and BB" = 2 x PB.
C.   Mark point C" on $\overrightarrow{PC}$, such that C is between P and C" and CC" = 2 x PC.
D.   Draw $\triangle A"B"C"$.

8.   a.   Is $\triangle ABC$ similar to $\triangle A"B"C"$? _____ Explain.

   b.   What is the scale factor? _____

   c.   What is the ratio of PA" to PA? _____

   d.   Trisect the sides of $\triangle A"B"C"$. Show how you could connect the trisection points to show that the area of $\triangle A"B"C"$ is nine times the area of $\triangle ABC$.

9.   a.   Is $\triangle A"B"C"$ similar to $\triangle A'B'C'$? _____

   b.   What is the scale factor? _____

   c.   What is the ratio of PA" to PA'? _____

   d.   How is the area of $\triangle A"B"C"$ related to the area of $\triangle A'B'C'$?

In Figure 2:

A. Draw rays $\overrightarrow{QA}$, $\overrightarrow{QB}$, and $\overrightarrow{QC}$.

B. Mark point X on $\overrightarrow{QA}$, such that A is between Q and X and QA = AX.

C. Mark point Y on $\overrightarrow{QB}$, such that B is between Q and Y and QB = BY.

D. Mark point Z on $\overrightarrow{QC}$, such that C is between Q and Z and QC = CZ.

E. Draw △XYZ.

10. a. Is △ABC similar to △XYZ? _____ Explain.

    b. What is the scale factor? _____

    c. What is the ratio of QX to QA? _____

    d. How is the area of △XYZ related to the area of △ABC? _____

    e. What effect does moving the similarity point have on the result of the transformation?

11. A dilation maps △JKL to △J'K'L'. If the similarity point is M:

    a. What is the scale factor of the dilation? _____

    b. How are the areas of the two triangles related? _____

II. OUTDOOR GEOMETRY

PURPOSE   This activity applies the properties of similar triangles to the problem of indirectly measuring heights or distances that are ordinarily inaccessible.

MATERIALS   For each group of three or four students:

- a mirror
- a 5 to10 meter measuring tape
- a straw
- a small washer
- a 40-cm length of thread
- 5 stakes and 100 meters of string or twine (optional)

REQUIRED BACKGROUND   Students should know:

- the properties of similar triangles
- how to write the ratios of the corresponding sides of similar triangles and solve a proportion
- how to write a proportion relating the sides of figures in a drawing
- the property of reflected light; that is, the angle of incidence is equal to the angle of reflection

TIME REQUIREMENT   50 to 60 minutes, depending on the number of objects to be measured

GETTING STARTED   Identify several tall or distant objects to be measured, such as a building, flag pole, tree, or football goal post. If simulating the measurement across a river or lake, you will need to mark the inaccessible points on either side of a street, a campus walk, or the like with stakes. Students will need the five stakes and string or twine to lay out triangles.

Students should work in teams of three or four. One may draw the figures and record the measurements, two can measure, and one can do the siting (as in the hypsometer or mirror method) or provide the shadow. Students should change roles so that each student performs each task at least once for the different activities. When reporting on the Inaccessible Points part of the activity, students should explain the method they used to determine the right angles.

Students at any level might be interested in an application of these methods in the short story "The Musgrave Ritual" from *The Memoirs of Sherlock Holmes* by Sir Arthur Conan Doyle. In the story, Holmes is faced with the problem of deciphering the riddle of the Musgrave ritual, which involves finding the length of the shadow of an elm tree at a certain time of day. Unfortunately, the tree has long since been cut down. As a youth, Holmes' client had been assigned the task of determining the height of that tree as part of his mathematics homework. He recalled that the tree was 64 feet tall.

Holmes then determined that a 6 foot fishing rod cast a 9 foot shadow at the appropriate time of day. In his usual way, he claimed, " The problem now is elementary, my dear Watson; if a rod of 6 feet has a shadow of 9 feet, a tree of 64 feet has a shadow of 96 feet." Using this story as an example and explaining Holmes' calculation provide an interesting introduction to the activity.

KEY IDEAS

Geometry is often taught without stressing its applications to the real world. This activity illustrates how properties of similar triangles can be applied outside the classroom. For example, a contractor may need to estimate the height of a building in need of repair, or a forester may need to estimate the amount of board feet of lumber in a stand of trees. Such real problems necessitate fairly accurate approximations. It should be emphasized that the final results are estimates and will only be as good as the accuracy of the measurements made while completing the activity.

When using the shadow method, remind students to measure the lengths of the shadows of the person and the object at the same time. One person's height and shadow length should not be measured and then used throughout the activity. As the day progresses, the length of a shadow changes.

IN THE CLASSROOM

Eighth-grade students who have studied similar triangles can do this activity. It may be advisable to have students use only one or two of the methods described, depending on their abilities.

If necessary, review the drawings on the activity pages so that students understand what measurements are to be made. Remind students that the distance from the eye level to the ground must be added to the height of the object when using the hypsometer method.

• **Activity**

OUTDOOR GEOMETRY

The methods described in this activity can be used to measure heights or distances that are not easily accessible. Each method is based on the fact that corresponding sides of similar triangles are proportional. One can construct two similar triangles, such that the distance to be determined is a side of one of the triangles. A proportion can then be written in which the unknown distance is one of the terms. The values of the other three terms, also lengths of sides of the triangles, can be measured and used to calculate the unknown distance.

SHADOW METHOD

Measure $\overline{NA}$, the height of a person, $\overline{AD}$, the length of the person's shadow, and $\overline{JI}$, the length of the shadow of the object whose height is being determined.

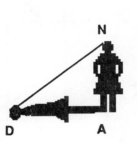

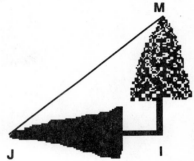

1.   Explain why $\triangle$ DAN ~ $\triangle$ JIM.

2.   Write the proportion that can be used to determine MI.

MIRROR METHOD

With a felt marker, draw a line connecting the midpoints of one pair of opposite sides of a mirror. Place the mirror on the ground so that the line is parallel to a line determined by placing a ruler on the toes of the shoes of a person facing the object to be measured, here represented by $\overline{EI}$. The person should look into the mirror and align the reflection of the top of the object to be measured (the house) with the line on the mirror represented by $\overline{RS}$. Point M is the intersection of $\overline{AI}$ and $\overline{RS}$. Measure $\overline{AM}$, $\overline{MI}$, and $\overline{EI}$. Note that $\overline{EI}$ is the eye-to-ground distance, *not* the height of the person. The point I should be located vertically below the person's eye (point E). If the person stands straight and does not lean over to look into the mirror, point I will be approximately at the toes of the shoes.

3.   Explain why $\triangle$ JAM ~ $\triangle$ EIM.

4.   Write a proportion that can be used to determine JA.

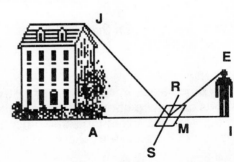

HYPSOMETER METHOD

To obtain the best results with this method, use a clipboard with a pad of paper attached to it. Pin a drinking straw along the top of the pad at C and B. Attach a small weight (a small washer or three paper clips) to one end of a 40 cm length of thread, and tie the other end of the thread to the pin at B. One person should hold the clipboard and site through the straw until the top of the object to be measured is sited. A second person should mark the point F on the edge of the pad to determine the ΔBAF. Measure $\overline{DC}$, $\overline{BA}$, $\overline{AF}$, and the distance from eye level to the ground.

5. Explain why ΔCDE ~ ΔBAF.

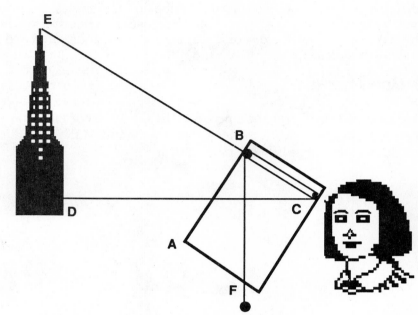

6. Write a proportion that could be used to determine DE.

7. What must be done to DE to determine the height of the building?

INACCESSIBLE POINTS

When surveying the boundaries of large tracts of land, it may be necessary to indirectly measure the distance between two points, such as the distance across a river (LI). A line $\overleftrightarrow{ID}$ is laid out along the edge of the river. Point L, a landmark on the opposite side of the river, is identified. Point I is located so that $\overline{LI} \perp \overleftrightarrow{ID}$, Point A is arbitrarily chosen, and point D is located on the line $\overleftrightarrow{ID}$ so that $\overline{DA} \perp \overleftrightarrow{ID}$. The line of site from A to L determines the point N on $\overleftrightarrow{ID}$. Points I, N, D, and A are marked with stakes. Measure $\overline{IN}$, $\overline{ND}$, and $\overline{DA}$.

8. Explain why Δ LIN ~ Δ ADN.

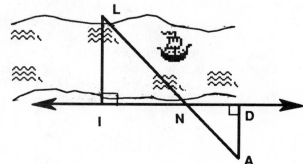

9. Write a proportion that could be used to determine LI.

Locate objects as directed by your instructor, and determine their measures. Use each of the methods described above at least once to measure an object. When possible, use different methods for measuring the same object, and compare the accuracy of your results. Make a separate drawing to show the similar triangles you used to determine each distance.

TRANSFORMATIONAL GEOMETRY

ACTIVITIES:
I. MOTION GEOMETRY

I. MOTION GEOMETRY

PURPOSE These activities introduce four geometric transformations – reflections, translations, rotations, and glide reflections. Students will explore the properties of each transformation and investigate concrete activities with the composition of functions. These activities also help develop spatial perception.

MATERIALS For each student:

- a compass
- a protractor
- a centimeter ruler
- a Mira
- one piece of tracing paper

REQUIRED BACKGROUND Students should:

- know how to measure angles and segments
- be familiar with the concepts of collinearity, betweenness, and congruence
- be able to construct the perpendicular bisector of a segment and the perpendicular from a given point to a given line

TIME REQUIREMENT
- Reflections: 50 to 60 minutes
- Reflections Revisited: 30 to 40 minutes
- Translations: 50 to 60 minutes
- Rotations: 70 to 80 minutes
- Glide Reflections: 30 to 40 minutes

GETTING STARTED For the most part, these activities are independent of one another. It is not essential to do them all or to do them in a particular order. However, students must be familiar with reflections to do the last three activities. The activities can be completed using just a straightedge and compass, but the necessary constructions are time consuming. The time requirements listed above are based on students using a Mira to perform the constructions.

Students should be instructed on the proper use of a Mira. Using a Mira provides a concrete representation of a reflection, focuses students' attention on the properties of the transformations, and decreases the time needed to complete the activities.

KEY IDEAS

REFLECTIONS Problems 1 through 3 develop the concept of a reflection, commonly referred to as a flip, and the fact that the reflecting line is the perpendicular bisector of the segment joining a point and its reflection image. This relationship is used in problem 6 to develop constructions for finding the reflection image of an object, given the reflecting line, and for finding the reflecting line, given a figure and its image. Problems 3b and 3c illustrate that a point is its own image if the point is on the reflecting line.

Reflections Revisited explores the properties of reflections. Since linear and angular measurements are preserved, a figure and its reflection must be congruent. However, the orientations of the figure and its image are reversed, as is seen in problem 9.

TRANSLATIONS The transformation that results from moving a figure through a fixed distance in a particular direction parallel to a given line is called a translation. The physical interpretation of this definition is developed in problem 1. Students see that the translation of a figure can be achieved by "sliding" it along congruent parallel segments or "tracks." Thus, translations are often called slides, and one way to specify a translation is to indicate the direction and the distance an object is to be moved.

Problem 1 also develops the notion that a translation is equivalent to the composite of two reflections through parallel lines. An object is always translated twice the distance between the reflecting lines, and the direction of motion is determined by the order in which the reflections are performed. If an object is translated by first reflecting it through line ℓ and then reflecting its image through line *m*, then the direction of motion is the direction that line ℓ must be moved to make it coincide with line *m*. Thus, a translation may also be specified by indicating two reflecting lines and the order in which the reflections are to be performed.

Since a translation is the composite of two reflections, it preserves collinearity, betweenness of points, the measure of segments and angles, and the orientation of a figure. Thus, a figure and its translation image must be congruent.

ROTATIONS In this activity, students should observe the connection between translations and rotations. A rotation is the result of sliding a figure along "tracks" that are arcs of concentric circles. The arcs subtend congruent central angles. For a translation, the "tracks" are congruent parallel segments.

A rotation, or turn, as it is often called, may be specified by indicating the center, direction, and magnitude of rotation. A translation is specified by stating the direction and magnitude. A rotation is the composite of two reflections through intersecting reflecting lines; for translations, the reflecting lines are parallel.

The magnitude of a rotation is always twice the measure of the acute angle formed by the reflecting lines, and the direction is determined by the order in which the reflections are performed. If an object is rotated by first reflecting it through line ℓ and then reflecting its image through line *m*, then the direction of the rotation is either clockwise or counterclockwise depending on whether line ℓ can be made to coincide with line *m* by rotating it clockwise or counterclockwise through an acute angle. Thus, a rotation may also be specified by indicating two reflecting lines and the order in which the reflections are to be performed. Again, note the duality between these latter statements and those for translations in the preceding section.

As with translations, rotations preserve collinearity, betweenness of points, the measure of segments and angles, and the orientation of a figure. Thus, a figure and its rotation image are congruent.

GLIDE REFLECTIONS   An isometry is a transformation that preserves the distance between points, so reflections, rotations, and translations are all isometries. Thus the concept of an isometry provides a unifying idea that ties the activities together. In this activity, students explore the properties of the only other isometry, a glide reflection.

EXTENSIONS

These activities may be extended to a study of transformations in the coordinate plane. This may be done by investigating such questions as:

- What is the image of the point P(0,5) when it is reflected through the line $y = 2x$?
- The point P(1,5) is the reflection of the point Q(3,3). What is the equation of the reflecting line?
- What is the image of the point S(2,1) when it is rotated 45° counterclockwise about the point R(1,2)?

This study may be further extended by using a computer graphing package or a graphing calculator to explore the relationship between the graphs of each of the following pairs of equations:

$$y = |x| \text{ and } y = |x - h| \qquad\qquad y = |x - h| \text{ and } y = |-x - h|$$
$$y = |x| \text{ and } y - k = |x| \qquad\qquad y = |x - h| \text{ and } -y = |x - h|$$
$$y = |x| \text{ and } y - k = |x - h|$$

The programs *Slide-Flip-Turn* from Level 6 and *Transformations* from Level 8 of the *Mathematics Activities Courseware* series published by Houghton Mifflin Publishing Company may also be used to extend the activities. These programs reinforce understanding of the transformations and provide practice identifying them.

Students may also be interested in exploring the use of isometries in the artwork of M. C. Escher. Several books on Escher's works are available from various publishers. Mira and Mira books are available from Creative Publications, Cuisenaire Company of America, and Dale Seymour Publications.

IN THE CLASSROOM

These activities may be adapted for use in grades 5 through 10. When used with students in grades 5 and 6, the ruler and compass constructions should be eliminated, and all transformations should be performed using a Mira. Regardless of the level, the activities require thorough discussion.

•Activity

REFLECTIONS

A Mira is a plastic drawing device that acts like a mirror that you can see through. A Mira reflects objects, just as a mirror does, but since the Mira is transparent, the image of an object reflected in it also appears behind the Mira.

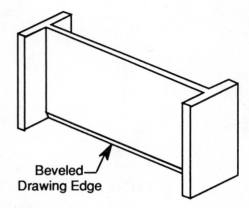

The drawing edge of a Mira is beveled. When using a Mira, it should be placed with the beveled edge down. Look directly through the Mira from the side with the beveled edge to locate the image of the object behind the Mira.

Beveled
Drawing Edge

1. Place your Mira so that the image of circle A fits on circle B. Hold the Mira steady with one hand, and draw a line along the drawing edge.

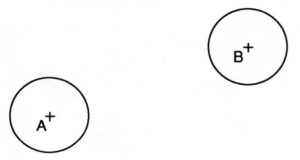

Take away the Mira. The line you have drawn is called the *Mira line*. It represents the Mira.

2. For each pair of figures below, fit the image of one of the figures onto the other, and draw the Mira line.

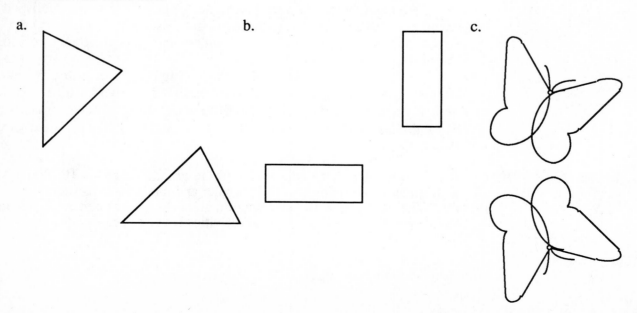

a.

b.

c.

Use a Mira to mark the location of the reflection of each point through line *ℓ*. Use prime notation to name each image point. For example, the image of point D would be named D'.

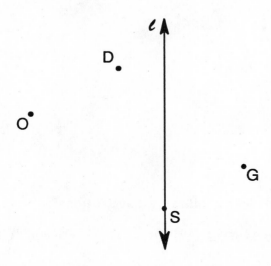

Draw line segments $\overline{DD'}$, $\overline{OO'}$, and $\overline{GG'}$. Label the points where line *ℓ* intersects these segments C, A, and T, respectively.

3.   a.   What is the relationship between the line *ℓ* and the segments $\overline{DD'}$, $\overline{OO'}$, and $\overline{GG'}$?

   b.   Where is point S located in relation to line *ℓ* ?

   c.   What is the relationship between points S and S'?

4.   Use a Mira to draw the reflection of each figure through the given line.

   a.

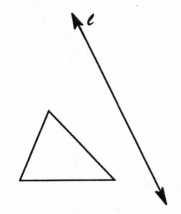

   b.

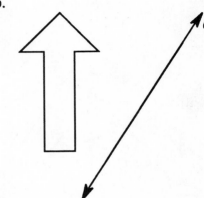

5.   Use a Mira to draw the reflection of each figure through the given line.

a.

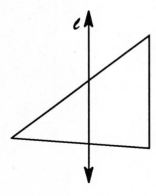

b.

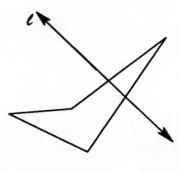

6.   Use a straightedge and compass to make the following constructions.

a.   A line *ℓ* so that point P is the reflection of point A through *ℓ*.

P •

• A

b.   A line *ℓ* so that pentagon R is the reflection of pentagon S through *ℓ*.

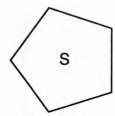

c.   The reflection of ΔABC through line *ℓ*.

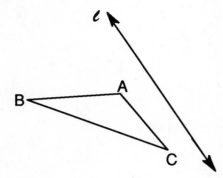

• **Looking Back**

REFLECTIONS REVISITED

Reflect the figure FLAG through the line ℓ. Use prime notation to label the reflection.

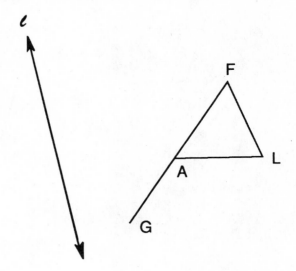

Measure the corresponding angles and segments in FLAG and its reflection image. Indicate the measures on the drawings.

7.   a.   Examine the measures of the angles. What do you conclude about the measure of an angle and the measure of its reflection?

     b.   Examine the lengths of the segments. What do you conclude about the length of a segment and the length of its reflection?

8.   Use your answers to problem 7 to help you complete the following statement: A triangle and its reflection through a line are _____.

9.   a.   Imagine tracing ΔFAL from F to A to L and back to F. What direction (clockwise or counterclockwise) do you move? _____.

     b.   Now trace the image ΔF'A'L' from F' to A' to L' and back to F'. What direction do you move? _____.

     c.   How does reflecting a figure through a line affect its orientation?

•Activity

TRANSLATIONS

1. a. Reflect △MAT through line ℓ_1. Use prime notation to label the reflection.

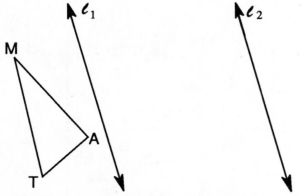

    b. Reflect △M'A'T' through line ℓ_2. Let M", A", and T" denote the images of M', A', and T', respectively.

    c. Draw $\overline{MM"}$, $\overline{AA"}$, and $\overline{TT"}$.

    d. Make a tracing of △MAT, and slide it onto △M"A"T" by moving its vertices along the three "tracks" you have just drawn. Is it necessary to flip or to turn the tracing to do this? _____

    e. What two relationships do the "tracks" appear to have?

The transformation in problem 1 is called a *translation*. The problem illustrates the following definition:

> *A translation is the composite of two reflections through parallel lines.*

2. a. Translate $\overline{ID}$ by reflecting it through line ℓ_3 and then reflecting the image through line ℓ_4. Let $\overline{ES}$ denote the final translation image of $\overline{ID}$.

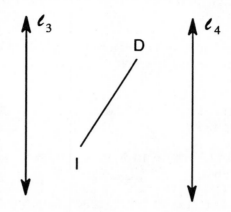

   b. What is the distance between lines ℓ_3 and ℓ_4? _____

   c. Measure the lengths IE and DS. How do these lengths compare with your answer in part b?

   d. In what direction was $\overline{ID}$ translated?

3.   a. Now translate $\overline{ID}$ by reflecting it through line ℓ_4 and then reflecting the image through line ℓ_3. Let $\overline{GL}$ denote the translation image of $\overline{ID}$.

   b. Measure the lengths IG and DL. How do these lengths compare with the result in 2b?

   c. In what direction was $\overline{ID}$ translated?

4.   a. If a point is translated by reflecting it through two parallel lines that are x units apart, what is the distance between the point and its translation image? _____

   b. If a figure is translated by first reflecting it through line ℓ_5 and then reflecting its image through line ℓ_6, in what direction will the figure be translated?

   c. Use the translation in problem 1 to check your conclusions in parts a and b.

5.   Which of the following are preserved by a translation? Explain your answers.

   a. collinearity of points

   b. betweenness of points

   c. angle measure

   d. distance between points

   e. orientation of a figure

   f. congruence of figures

•Activity

ROTATIONS

You have studied two basic geometric transformations, reflections and translations. The drawings in Figure 1 illustrate a third transformation. The two figures are identical, but the duck is neither a reflection nor a translation of the rabbit. *Use a Mira to verify that the duck is not a reflection of the rabbit and a tracing of the duck to verify that it is not a translation.*

To illustrate the relationship between the rabbit and the duck, place a piece of tracing paper over the rabbit, and pin it at point P. Trace the rabbit, then turn the paper about the pin until the rabbit coincides with the duck. This should explain why the duck is called a *rotation image* of the rabbit.

P.

Figure 1

Reflections can also be used to illustrate the relationship between the rabbit and the duck. The drawings in Figure 2 show that, if the rabbit, R_1, is reflected through line ℓ_1, and if its image, R_2, is reflected through line ℓ_2, then the result is the duck, R_3. *Verify this with your Mira.*

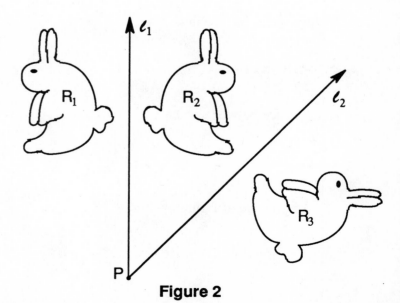

Figure 2

As the preceding example shows, the rotation that transforms the rabbit into the duck is the composite of two reflections through intersecting lines. This illustrates the following definitions:

> *A rotation is the composite of two reflections through intersecting lines.*
> *The center of rotation is the point at which the two lines intersect.*

1. What is the measure of the acute angle formed by lines ℓ_1 and ℓ_2 below? _____

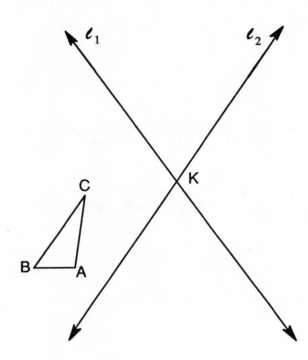

2. Rotate △ABC by reflecting it through line ℓ_1 and then reflecting its image through line ℓ_2. Let X, Y, and Z be the rotation images of points A, B, and C, respectively.

   a. Draw and measure ∠BKY. _____

   Note that the vertex of ∠BKY is at the center of rotation and that one side of the angle contains a point B on the original figure; the other side contains the rotation image, Y, of the point B. The measure of an angle formed this way is called the *magnitude of the rotation*.

   b. How does the magnitude of the rotation compare with your answer to problem 1?

   c. In what direction, clockwise or counterclockwise, was △ABC rotated?

3. Now rotate △ABC by reflecting it through line ℓ_2 and then reflecting its image through line ℓ_1. Let R, S, and T be the rotation images of points A, B, and C, respectively.

    a. What is the magnitude of the rotation? _____
        How does it compare with your answer to problem 1?

    b. In what direction was △ABC rotated? _____

4. a. On the figure in problem 1, draw three circles with center K and radii BK, CK, and AK, respectively. What do you notice about the circles?

    b. Make a tracing of △ABC, and slide it onto △XYZ by moving its vertices along the three "tracks" you have just drawn. Is it necessary to flip or to turn the tracing to do this? _____

5. a. A point is rotated by reflecting it through two intersecting lines which form an acute angle with measure $x°$. What will the magnitude of the rotation be?

    b. If a figure is rotated by first reflecting it through line ℓ_3 and then reflecting its image through line ℓ_4, in what direction will the figure be rotated?

    c. Use the rabbit-duck rotation to check your conclusions in parts a and b.

6. Which of the following are preserved by a rotation? Explain your answers.

    a. collinearity of points

    b. betweenness of points

    c. angle measure

    d. distance between points.

    e. orientation of a figure

    f. congruence of figures

•Activity

GLIDE REFLECTIONS

In Figure 1, footprint F_3 is a *glide reflection* of footprint F_1. As the name suggests, a glide reflection is a glide (or translation) followed by a reflection. However, *the reflecting line must be parallel to the direction of the glide.*

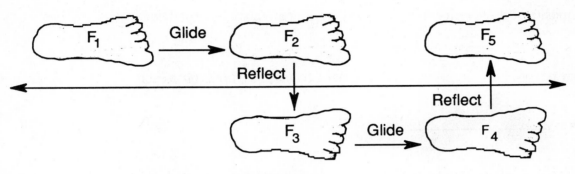

Figure 1

1. A glide reflection maps $\triangle ABC$ onto $\triangle A'B'C'$. Draw segments $\overline{AA'}$, $\overline{BB'}$, and $\overline{CC'}$, and find their midpoints. What appears to be true about the midpoints of the segments?

2. A glide reflection maps $\triangle XYZ$ onto $\triangle X'Y'Z'$. Find the reflecting line, and draw the glide image of $\triangle XYZ$.

3. Study Figure 1. What single transformation is equivalent to the result of using a glide reflection twice? _____

4.   Complete the following statements:

   a.   The composite of two reflections through parallel lines is a _____.

   b.   The composite of two reflections through intersecting lines is a _____.

   c.   The composite of three reflections through parallel lines is a _____.

   d.   The composite of three reflections through concurrent lines is a _____.

   e.   The composite of three reflections through lines that are not all parallel and not all concurrent is a _____.

5.   Identify the transformation that will map the shaded hawk in Figure 2 onto each lettered hawk.

   a.   Hawk A _____

   b.   Hawk B _____

   c.   Hawk C _____

   d.   Hawk D _____

   e.   Hawk E _____

   f.   Hawk F _____

Figure 2

PERIMETER AND AREA

ACTIVITIES:
I. PICK'S THEOREM
II. RIGHT OR NOT?

I. PICK'S THEOREM

PURPOSE
This activity reinforces the concept of area and applies the patterns problem solving strategy to determine a rule for finding the area of a polygon constructed on a geoboard or on square dot paper. Students' calculations of the area of a specific polygon with no grid points inside the figure are extended to any polygon that might be constructed on the grid. The activity reinforces the concept of dividing a figure into smaller nonoverlapping polygons in order to determine the area of the original polygon. By doing so, the activity also reinforces the concept of conservation of area.

MATERIALS
For each student:

- a geoboard and rubber bands
- square dot paper

REQUIRED BACKGROUND
Students should know:

- the concept of area
- how to determine the area of a polygon by dividing the figure into squares or fractions of squares
- how to develop a rule to describe a linear sequence

TIME REQUIRMENT
30 to 40 minutes

GETTING STARTED
It would be helpful to students if they have completed the Constant Differences and What's the Rule? activities in Chapter 1 so that they are familiar with the idea of developing a rule to describe a linear sequence. Remind students that the area of the smallest square that can be constructed on a geoboard or on grid paper has an area of *one* square unit. If students construct the polygons on a geoboard, the results should be recorded on dot paper so they have their results to refer back to if necessary. In the first part of the activity, all polygons must be constructed with *no* points inside the figure. Students should derive a rule for determining the area of a polygon in relation to the number of grid points on the perimeter of the polygon before going on to the second part of the activity.

KEY IDEAS   When asked "What is area?"students commonly respond "length times width" or " base times altitude." Students often miss the fundamental idea of area as a covering because their experience with area has usually focused on formulas for computing the area of specific polygons. Throughout this activity, to determine area, students may simply count squares as they partition a polygon. By doing so, they focus on the square as a unit of area and on the total area of a polygon as the sum of its various parts rather than focusing on the result of applying a formula. Thus, the covering concept of area is constantly reinforced.

To determine the area of a polygon whose sides are not horizontal or vertical segments, students may find it easier to construct a rectangle around the outside of the polygon, determine the area of the rectangle, and then subtract the area of the regions that are outside the given polygon.

In the Looking Back activity, if students are not given any direction, they will often construct figures with a random number of points on the perimeter and inside the figure. Because of this random procedure, students may not be able to recognize the pattern relating the area to the points. The directions have been structured so that students first construct polygons with one point inside, then two points inside, and so on. If students will then organize their data in the table by ordering the number of points on the perimeter and the number of points inside, they will be more likely to discover the pattern. Review and stress this strategy during the class discussion following the activity.

While discussing Pick's Theorem Revisited, the use of two important steps from Polya's problem solving model should be stressed:

A. One should ask the question, "Have I seen a problem like this before that may be of some help?"
B. If so, can I use the results or solution of the previous problem to assist in the solution of this problem?

In this activity, students will discover that:

the rule for Pick's Theorem is $A = 1/2\,N_p - 1$

the rule for Pick's Theorem Revisited is $A = 1/2\,N_p - 1 + N_i$

where A = the area of a polygon formed on a geoboard or on square grid paper
N_p = the number of points on the perimeter of the polygon
N_i = the number of points in the interior of the polygon

EXTENSIONS   Triangular, pentagonal, or hexagonal grid paper can be used to extend this activity. Students will be forced to rethink their concept of area when the triangle, pentagon, or hexagon is now the unit of area. Again, students should first construct polygons without any points inside the figure and then determine a formula that relates the area to the number of points on the perimeter. The process should then be repeated with polygons that contain points in the interior. Partitioning the polygons will force students to develop new strategies to determine the areas of the parts of the original figure.

IN THE CLASSROOM   This activity is appropriate for students in grades 5 through 8 when area is being studied. As described in the Required Backround section, they should also know how to develop a rule to describe a linear sequence. Since the activity requires no specific formula for determining area, it provides a good opportunity to reinforce the concept of area and strategies for dividing a complex area into smaller units. Students at this age conserve number, but many have not developed the concept of conservation of area. The partitioning and combining of smaller areas to determine total area will help to develop and reinforce this concept.

• Activity
_____

PICK'S THEOREM

For the purpose of this activity, the area of the smallest square that can be constructed by connecting four points on your geoboard or on dot paper is *one* unit.

1. For each of the polygons shown, count the number of points on the perimeter, find the area, and enter the results in the table below.

a.

Area = 1   Area = _____

b.

Area = _____

c.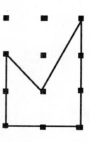

Area = _____

d.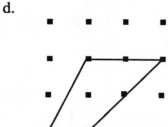

Area = _____

e.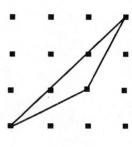

Area = _____

On your geoboard or on dot paper, construct several other polygons in which no points are in the interior. Compute the area of each polygon, and record the results in the table.

Number of Points on the Perimeter (N_p)	3	4	5	6	7			
Area of the Polygon (A)		1						

2. Look for a pattern in the data in the table. Write a rule that relates the area of a polygon (A) to the number of points on the perimeter of the polygon (N_p).

• Looking Back

PICK'S THEOREM REVISITED

3. a. On your geoboard or grid paper, construct three different polygons that have one point in the interior of the figure.

    b. Count the number of points (N_p) on the perimeter of each polygon and the number of points (N_i) inside. Then determine the area (A) and record your data in the table below.

    c. Now construct some other polygons that have two points in the interior of the figure. Count the points on the perimeter and inside the figure as above, then determine the area for each.

    d. Continue this procedure, constructing polygons with three and four points inside the figure. Determine the area for each polygon, and record the data for each polygon in the table.

Number of Points on the Perimeter (N_p)								
Number of Points in the Perimeter (N_i)								
Area of the Polygon (A)								

4. Examine the data in the table. Write a rule that relates the area of the polygon (A) to the number of points on the perimeter (N_p) and the number of points in the interior of the polygon (N_i).

II. RIGHT OR NOT?

PURPOSE   This activity can be used to develop the Pythagorean Theorem and its converse. The activity also explores the relationship between the lengths of the sides of a triangle and its classification as an acute, right, or obtuse triangle. Students who have already been introduced to the Pythagorean Theorem will discover the generalization of the theorem to other kinds of triangles.

MATERIALS   For each pair of students:

- centimeter grid paper
- scissors
- a protractor

REQUIRED BACKGROUND   Students should know:

- how to measure angles
- the classifications of triangles by type of angle

TIME REQUIREMENT   30 to 40 minutes

GETTING STARTED   Students should work in pairs so that they can share their results as they construct the triangles. Instruct them to cut out the squares from grid paper as illustrated on the first activity page, construct several triangles, measure the angles in the triangles as needed, and complete Table 1. Since students need only know if an angle is larger or smaller than a right angle, they can use the corner of a piece of paper for comparison.

    Students should complete Table 2 using the data from Table 1. They can then complete the statements below Table 2 that generalize the relationship between the lengths of the sides of any triangle and its classification according to angle.

KEY IDEAS   Class discussion should focus on the fact that each triangle was constructed by placing squares together as indicated and that the lengths of the sides of each triangle are the same as the lengths of the sides of the squares. By using this modeling approach with students when introducing the Pythagorean Theorem, students can make the connection between the lengths of the sides of the triangle, the area of the squares used to construct the sides, and the squares of the lengths of the sides of the triangle. When presented with an example, such as

$$3^2 + 4^2 = 5^2$$

$$9 + 16 = 25,$$

students have no model by which they can relate 3^2 to the area of a square with a side of 3 or understand that the 3^2 is also related to the square that can be constructed on one side of a right triangle. By constructing triangles using squares, students are more apt to make a firm connection between the geometric concept of a square and the square of the length of the side of a triangle.

Most students who study geometry from the middle school level on are exposed to the Pythagorean Theorem; many also see its converse. Rarely, if ever, do students study the relationship between the lengths of the sides of acute or obtuse triangles. Many students can readily state that a triangle with sides of lengths of 3, 4, and 5 is a right triangle, but few if any students would know the classification of a triangle with sides of 7, 12, and 15. Following this activity, students should be able to classify any triangle, given the measures of the three sides.

During the class discussion, ask students if they selected three squares that did not form a triangle, and have them give examples. This question will reinforce the triangle inequality theorem; that is, the sum of the measures of any two sides of a triangle is greater than the measure of the third side.

EXTENSIONS Numerous materials are available for exploring the world of the Pythagorean Theorem, its many proofs, and its fascinating history. One extension of this activity that demonstrates the connection between the theorem and geometric construction is to investigate the relationship between the areas of regular polygons constructed on the sides of a right triangle.

Using a compass, students can easily construct equilateral triangles on each side of a given right triangle, as shown below. Using the formula for the area of an equilateral triangle, students can determine the area of each triangle and show that the sum of the areas of the two smaller triangles is equal to the area of the largest triangle.

$$A = \frac{s^2}{4}\sqrt{3}$$

$$A = \frac{8^2}{4}\sqrt{3} = 16\sqrt{3}$$

$$A = \frac{6^2}{4}\sqrt{3} = 9\sqrt{3}$$

$$A = \frac{10^2}{4}\sqrt{3} = 25\sqrt{3}$$

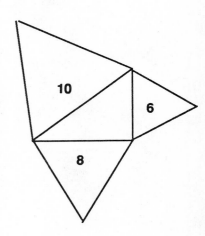

The construction of a regular hexagon is also simple, and the area of a regular hexagon is easily determined by dividing it into six equilateral triangles.

For the general case of a regular polygon, the formula $A = 1/2\ ap$ may be applied, where a is the apothem of the polygon and p is the perimeter. Students can discover that the area of any regular polygon constructed on the hypotenuse of a triangle is equal to the sum of the areas of the similar regular polygons constructed on the other two sides.

IN THE CLASSROOM

This activity is appropriate for use in grades 7 and 8, where the Pythagorean Theorem is most often introduced. It may be used to develop the theorem, reinforce it if previously taught, and generalize the theorem to other triangles.

Students may have some difficulty placing the squares together to form the triangles and determining the measures of the angles. Pairing students helps promote the cooperative learning process and eliminates this problem.

An excellent videotape on the Pythagorean Theorem, entitled *The Theorem of Pythagoras*, is available from Project Mathematics at the California Institue of Technology in Pasadena, California. The film explores several methods of proof of the theorem, many of which are illustrated with graphic composition and decompostion of various figures.

• Activity

RIGHT OR NOT?

1. A. From a sheet of grid paper, cut out squares with areas of 9, 16, 25, 36, 49, 64, 81, 100, 121, 144, and 169 square units.

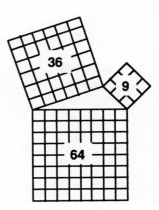

B. Use three of the squares to construct a triangle as shown at the right.

C. Measure the angles of the triangle thus formed to determine if the triangle is acute, right, or obtuse. Enter the data in Table 1.

D. Use sets of three squares to build other triangles, and enter the data in Table 1.

TABLE 1

Area of the Largest Square	Area of the Smallest Square	Area of the Third Square	Sum of the Area of the Two Smaller Squares	Is the Triangle Acute, Right, or Obtuse?
64	9	36	45	obtuse
100	36	64		
36	16	25		
169				
121				
144				

2. Complete Table 2 using your data from Table 1. Record the measures of the lengths of the sides of the triangles

TABLE 2

Length of Longest Side of Triangle	Square of Length of Longest Side	Length of Shortest Side of Triangle	Length of Third Side of Triangle	Sum of the Squares of the Two Shorter Sides	Is the Triangle Acute, Right, or Obtuse?
8	64	3	6	45	obtuse

3. Use the data from Table 2 to complete the following statements:

   a. If the square of the length of the longest side of a triangle *is less than* the sum of the squares of the lengths of the two shorter sides, the triangle is a(n) _____ triangle.

   b. If the square of the length of the longest side of a triangle *is equal to* the sum of the squares of the lengths of the two shorter sides, the triangle is a(n) _____ triangle.

   c. If the square of the length of the longest side of a triangle *is greater than* the sum of the squares of the lengths of the two shorter sides, the triangle is a(n) _____ triangle.

COORDINATE GEOMETRY

ACTIVITIES:
I. MYSTERIOUS MIDPOINTS
II. RECTANGLES AND CURVES

I. MYSTERIOUS MIDPOINTS

PURPOSE In this activity, students apply coordinate geometry techniques to reinforce their understanding of the properties of quadrilaterals. This activity also reinforces coordinate graphing and understanding of the theorem stating that a line segment that connects the midpoints of two sides of a triangle is parallel to the third side and its length is one-half the length of the third side.

MATERIALS   For each student:

- graph paper
- a ruler

REQUIRED BACKGROUND   Students should know:

- how to plot points on a coordinate graph
- how to determine the slope of a line and the distance between two points
- the theorem regarding a segment connecting the midpoints of two sides of a triangle

TIME REQUIREMENT   40 to 50 minutes

GETTING STARTED   Students should complete the Classifying Triangles and Classifying Quadrilaterals activities in Chapter 10 prior to doing this activity. After students have completed this activity individually, they can compare results in small groups to verify and evaluate their conjectures. No special instructions are needed unless students are not familiar with the material in the Required Background section.

KEY IDEAS   Students can verify that the quadrilateral formed by joining the midpoints of the sides of any quadrilateral (or the quadrilateral formed by extending the sides, as described in the Extensions section) is a special quadrilateral. Students should determine the slopes and measures of the line segments, compare these results to determine parallel and congruent sides, and apply the properties of quadrilaterals to determine what type of quadrilateral is formed.

Prior to determining the ratio of the area of the original quadrilateral to the area of the parallelogram formed by connecting the midpoints of the four sides, students should first be asked to predict the result.

After discovering that this ratio is 1 to 2, students may then assume that the same result will hold true when the sides are extended and a quadrilateral is formed. However, they should be able to determine the relationship among the areas of the five polygons that comprise the large quadrilateral formed by this construction and then show that the area of the original quadrilateral is one-fifth of the area of the new figure.

EXTENSIONS   Computer software offers an alternate method for exploring the problems in this activity and a means of verifying the conjectures made by students. Programs like *The Geometric Supposer* from Sunburst Communications allow students to draw the figures, locate the midpoints, measure the lengths of segments, and determine areas. Students should explore a variety of figures like those given in problems 1 and 4 and verify that their completed statements in problem 7 apply to all the figures they constructed.

Students should also use the software to find the areas of the original quadrilateral and the one formed by connecting the midpoints and then determine the ratio of the two areas. Having made a conjecture about the ratio of the areas, they should then verify the result using coordinate methods with the problems in the activity. Finally, they should develop a proof to justify their statements.

A second set of explorations can be developed by having students extend each side of a quadrilateral in order, connect the endpoints of the segments, and investigate the properties of the new quadrilateral. For example, given quadrilateral ABCD, students should extend $\overline{AB}$ through B to Q, $\overline{BC}$ through C to M, $\overline{CD}$ through D to N, and $\overline{DA}$ through A to P so that in each case the extension is the same length as the side of the quadrilateral that was extended. Then students can draw the quadrilateral MNPQ.

Students should first conjecture about what type of quadrilateral will be formed and then explore such questions as:

- Do you ever get the same type of quadrilateral as the original?
- Can you always predict what quadrilateral will result?
- What happens when you begin with a concave quadrilateral?
- If a quadrilateral is formed by extending the sides as described above, are the sides of the resulting figure twice the length of the sides of the original figure?
- What is the ratio of the area of the original quadrilateral to the area of the new figure formed by this construction?

This last question should first be explored using computer software. Once conjectures have been made, proofs of statements should be developed through coordinate and synthetic means.

IN THE CLASSROOM   Most of this activity can be completed by eighth-grade students or even by seventh graders, if they have sufficient background in coordinate geometry. We would expect all students at this level to be able to draw the quadrilateral, connect the midpoints, and draw the resulting figure. Many students may be able to identify the resulting quadrilateral and complete the statements in problem 7, but some may lack the background to verify their conjectures or to formulate a proof. A carefully guided discussion may be necessary for students to understand the relationship between the quadrilateral formed by connecting the midpoints and the properties of the original figure.

• Activity

MYSTERIOUS MIDPOINTS

1. On a sheet of graph paper, draw each of the following quadrilaterals by plotting the points and connecting them in order. Draw each figure on a separate set of coordinate axes.

    a. P (2,5), I (4,2), N (13,1), K (7,8)   b. B (-1,-5), R (4,2), O (0,0), W (-4,5)

    c. R (5,-1), O (-3,-1), S (-6,-5), E (5,-5)   d. P (11,3), O (11,8), L (2,4), Y (0,0)

2. Mark the midpoints of the sides of each quadrilateral, and label them consecutively M, A, T, H. Connect the points to form another quadrilateral. What appears to be true about each of the polygons MATH?

3. Explain how you can check your conjecture. Find the slopes of the segments and their lengths to check your conjecture.

4. On a sheet of graph paper, draw the following by plotting the points and connecting them in order. Draw each figure on a separate set of coordinate axes.

    a. D (4,8), U (1,3), C (10,6), K (13,11)   b. B (2,-2), I (9,1), K (2,4), E (-5,1)

    c. D (2,3), A (-3,3), V (-3,-4), E (2,-4)   d. P (-2,-5), I (-7,0), C (-2,5), K (3,0)

5. Locate the midpoints of the sides, and label them consecutively M, O, N, T. Connect the points to form quadrilaterals.

    a. Are any of the MONT quadrilaterals special quadrilaterals? _____

    b. Are any of them the same type of quadrilateral as the original figure? _____
        If so, which one(s)?
        _____

6. In each of the MONT quadrilaterals in problem 5, locate the midpoints of the sides, label them consecutively W, X, Y, Z, and connect them in order to form new quadrilaterals. How are the new WXYZ quadrilaterals related to the original figures given in problem 4?

7. Complete each of the following statements.

    a. If you connect the midpoints of a quadrilateral in order, the resulting figure is a _____.

    b. If you connect the midpoints of a rectangle in order, the resulting figure is a _____.

    c. If you connect the midpoints of a rhombus in order, the resulting figure is a _____.

    d. If you connect the midpoints of a square in order, the resulting figure is a _____.

8. Explain which properties of the original quadrilateral determine which new special quadrilateral is formed by connecting the midpoints of the sides.

II. RECTANGLES AND CURVES

PURPOSE   This activity reinforces the concepts of perimeter and area and illustrates three different displays of the same data, a pictograph, a graph of discrete data, and a graph of continuous data. The activity also develops the concept of a limit by graphically illustrating that there is a minimum perimeter that encloses a given area and a maximum area enclosed by a given perimeter.

MATERIALS   For each student:

- graph or dot paper
- scissors
- 36 square chips or tiles (optional)
- a loop of string 24 cm in circumference (optional)

REQUIRED BACKGROUND   Students should know:

- the concepts of area and perimeter
- how to construct rectangles with integral dimensions, given the area or the perimeter
- how to determine the possible dimensions of a rectangle, given the area or the perimeter
- how to locate points on a coordinate graph and how to construct a graph to represent a set of data

TIME REQUIREMENT   70 to 80 minutes

GETTING STARTED   Students may work in groups of two to four so that they can share results as they determine the rectangles. Students can combine results to construct the pictograph, but each student should make a drawing of the completed pictograph. It may be necessary to point out that two rectangles may be congruent and yet be represented by two different ordered pairs, such as (3,12) and (12,3), in which the coordinates represent the lengths of the base and height, respectively. In this activity, two such congruent rectangles will be considered as different and distinct. It is important for students to determine all the possible rectangles with integral dimensions as they complete each table.

KEY IDEAS   This activity develops some important concepts of advanced mathematics but in an introductory manner using concrete models and a graphic approach. Students should recognize the connection between the pictograph and Graph 1. The pictograph uses the actual rectangles and is a physical display of the data. Graph 1 illustrates the dimensions of the rectangles, yet the nine points still display the same visual image as the pictograph. It is important for students to understand that each of these graphs represents data only for the nine rectangles that were constructed. Many other rectangles with an area of 36 are not included in these graphs. These graphs illustrate discrete data.

In Graph 2, data for all possible rectangles are included, and now we have a graph of continuous data. Students should explore the inverse relationship in which the base increases and the height decreases, yet the area remains constant. The curve approaches either axis. Thus, as the base or height increases, the other dimension approaches zero as a limit. Each axis is an *asymptote* to the curve. The concept of limit should be the focal point of the discussion here and later in the activity.

Graph 3 again illustrates the concept of limit. There is a rectangle, a 6 x 6 square, with a minimum perimeter and an area of 36. Students should recognize that, for a given area, there is no limit to the maximum perimeter that will enclose it.

In the second part of the activity, the perimeter is fixed. Students may be surprised to see that Graph 4 differs considerably from Graph 1. During class discussion, attention should be given to the two equations $A = bh$ and $P = 2b + 2h$, the degree of each, the relationship between the graphs and the equations, and the reason why the first equation results in a curve and the second equation results in a line.

Graph 5 also illustrates the concept of limit; however, in this case, students should discover that there is a maximum area that can be enclosed with a given perimeter of 24 and that the area approaches zero as a minimum. Students should recognize that the lines whose equations are $b = 0$ and $b = 12$ are two asymptotes to the curve. The relationship between the maximum and minimum values for b seen in this graph should be explored in Graph 4. Students should realize that, if the line did intercept the axes in Graph 4, then the resulting rectangles would have an area of zero.

In summary, students should discover the inverse relationship between area and perimeter. Given a rectangle with a fixed area, there is a minimum perimeter but no maximum perimeter that will enclose it. However, given a fixed perimeter for a rectangle, there is a maximum area that can be enclosed, and the area approaches zero as a minimum.

EXTENSIONS

The logical extension to this activity is to explore what figure with an area of 36 has the least perimeter. Or, given a perimeter of 24, what is the maximum area that can be enclosed, and by what figure?

In the activity, students discover that the rectangle that encloses the maximum area is a square. Given the perimeter of 24, is there another polygon of greater area? If a regular hexagon has a perimeter of 24, then one side is 4. The hexagon can be partitioned into six nonoverlapping equilateral triangles. Students can determine the area of the hexagon using the formula for the area of an equilateral triangle and compare the result with the area of the square they determined in the activity. Using some estimation, they can then divide the hexagon into a regular dodecagon, find the area of one of the 12 nonoverlapping triangles, and thus determine the area of a regular dodecagon whose perimeter is 24.

This activity should lead students to explore the relationship between the area and the circumference of a circle. First, find the area of a circle with a circumference of 24, and compare this result with the areas of the square determined in the second part of the activity and the regular hexagon and regular dodecagon suggested above. Then, determine the circumference of a circle whose area is 36, and compare the result with the perimeter of the square found in the first part of the activity.

IN THE CLASSROOM

This activity provides a connection between area, perimeter, and graphing data for seventh or eighth graders after these topics have been studied. The formulas for area and perimeter and the graphs of the equations comprise the focus of the activity and provide the setting in which the concept of a limit is introduced. Thus, it may be appropriate to use this activity during a section in algebra when graphing functions. Both linear and quadratic functions are included. The two different graphs of quadratic functions and the graph of the linear function provide students with the opportunity to explore the differences among the equations and the resulting differences among the graphs.

• Activity

RECTANGLES AND CURVES

Given a set of 36 squares, determine *all* possible rectangles that can be constructed using *all* the squares. As you determine each rectangle, outline it on a piece of graph paper or dot paper and label the base and the height. Record the base (b), the height (h), and the perimeter (P) for each rectangle in Table 1.

TABLE 1

AREA = 36								
Base (*b*)								
Height (*h*)								
Perimeter (*P*)								

1. Cut out each rectangle. Construct a graph showing only the first quadrant. Label the horizontal axis b and the vertical axis h. Place each rectangle on the axis, as illustrated in the graph at the right. Each rectangle must be placed such that one vertex is at (0,0). This graph is called a pictograph. Make a drawing of the completed pictograph.

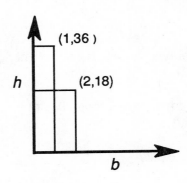

2. Using the data in Table 1, plot the ordered pairs (*b*,*h*) that represent the base and height of each rectangle in Graph 1.

GRAPH 1

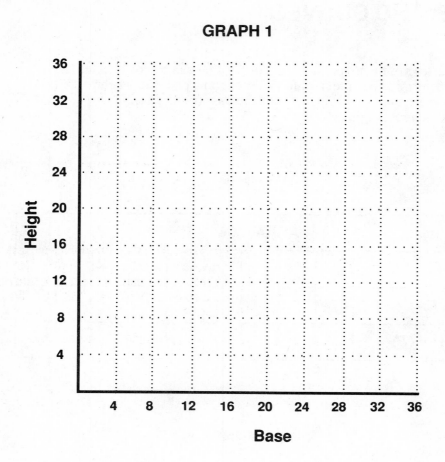

Base

The data displayed in Graph 1 represent *all* rectangles that can be constructed using 36 squares.

3. Are there any other rectangles with an area of 36? _____

4. How many exist? _____

5. List the dimensions of at least three other rectangles whose area is 36.

6. Are these rectangles represented in Graph 1? _____ If not, describe where on the graph the new points should be placed.

On Graph 2, plot and connect the points that represent the ordered pairs (b,h)
for *all* possible rectangles whose area is 36. (Hint: Use the points on Graph 1.)

GRAPH 2

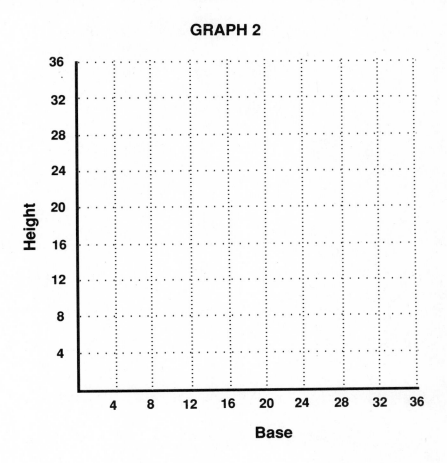

7. Will the graph of these data intersect either axis? _____
   If so, where? _____   If not, explain.

8. Can any point on the graph lie below the horizontal axis? _____
   Explain.

Using the data from Table 1, plot the ordered pairs (b, P) on Graph 3. Connect the points on the graph with a smooth curve.

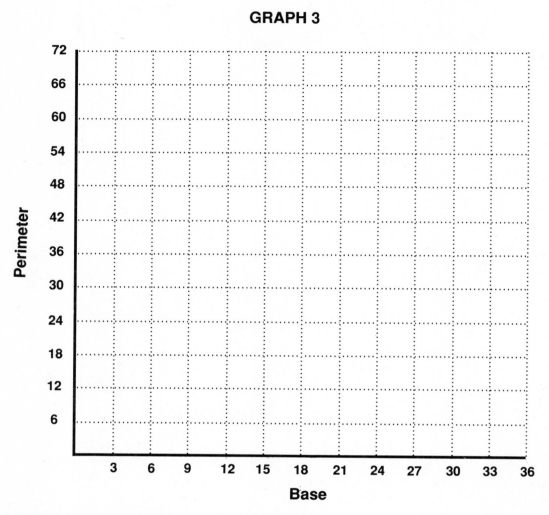

GRAPH 3

9.   Each rectangle represented on the graph has an area of _____ .

10. What is the least perimeter of any rectangle? _____

11. What are the dimensions of the rectangle with least perimeter? _____

12. Is there a rectangle with a greatest perimeter? _____ Explain.

13. The area of all rectangles represented on the graph is 36. Explain how it is possible for a rectangle to have an area of 36, yet have a perimeter that is unlimited.

14. Describe a physical model that you could use to illustrate the concept of a finite area being enclosed by an unlimited perimeter.

Given a loop of string 24 cm in circumference, determine *all* possible rectangles with integral dimensions that can be enclosed by the loop on centimeter graph or dot paper. As you determine each rectangle, outline it on a piece of graph paper or dot paper, and label the base and the height. Record the base (b), the height (h), and the area (A) for each rectangle in Table 2.

TABLE 2

Perimeter = 24											
Base (b)											
Height (h)											
Area (A)											

15. Using the data in Table 2, plot the ordered pairs (b,h) that represent the base and height of each rectangle in Graph 4. Draw a line through the points.

GRAPH 4

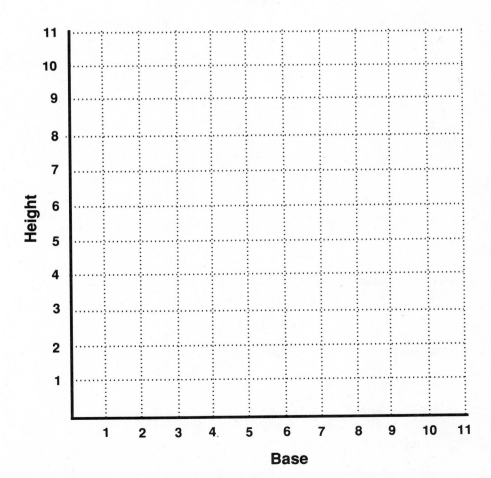

Graph 4 displays the data for *all* rectangles with a perimeter of 24 cm.

16. Will the graph of these data intersect either axis? _____   If so, where? _____

17. If the line did intersect the horizontal axis (*b*), what would be the coordinate of that point? _____ Explain the relationship between the coordinate (*b*) of that point and the perimeter.

Using the data from the Table 2, plot the ordered pairs (*b*, *A*) on Graph 5. Connect the points on the graph with a smooth curve.

GRAPH 5

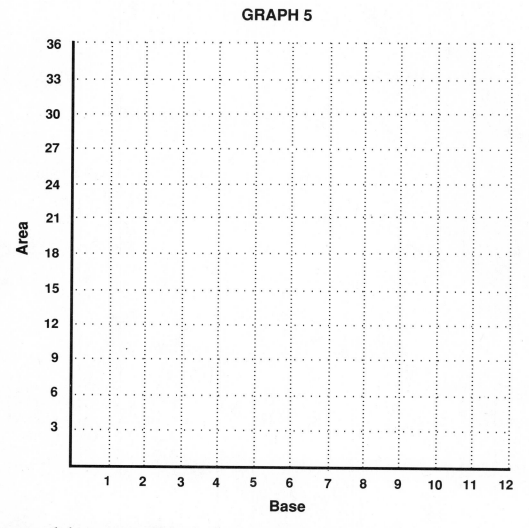

18. If a rectangle has an area of 24, what is the measure of the base? _____

19. What is the maximum area of any rectangle? _____

20. What are the dimensions of the rectangle with maximum area? _____

21. Is there a rectangle with a least area? _____ Explain.

22. As the area of the rectangle approaches zero, the measure of the base approaches a maximum value of _____. Explain.

ANSWERS

CHAPTER 1: PROBLEM SOLVING

MAKING SEQUENCES

1.	14,	17,	20,	23,	26			
2.	28,	33,	38,	43,	48			
3.	25,	18,	11,	4,	-3			
4.	16,	22,	29,	37,	46			
5.	28,	39,	52,	67,	84			
6.	4,	10,	16,	22,	28,	34,	40,	46
7.	44,	41,	38,	35,	32,	29,	26,	23
8.	6,	13,	32,	69,	130,	221,	348,	517
9.	2,	12,	36,	80,	150,	252,	392,	576

CONSTANT DIFFERENCES 1. a. Constant difference = 7, 10th Term = 67, 50th Term = 347
b. Rule : 7 x Term Number - 3 2. Constant difference = -5, 10th Term = -19
3. Rule : -5 x Term Number + 31

WHAT'S THE RULE?

					Rule	97th Term	423rd Term
1.	25,	29,	33,	37	4T + 5	393	1697
2.	2,	3,	4,	5	1T - 3	94	420
3.	57,	67,	77,	87	10T + 7	977	4237
4.	90,	88,	86,	84	-2T + 100	-94	-746
5.	23,	28,	33,	38	5T - 2	483	2113
6.	556,	553,	550,	547	-3T + 571	280	-698
7.	25,	31,	37,	43	6T - 5	577	2533
8.	173,	165,	157,	149	-8T + 213	-563	-3171
9.	46,	53,	60,	67	7T + 11	690	2972
10.	644,	635,	626,	617	-9T + 689	-184	-3118
11.	30,	37,	44,	51	7T - 5	674	2956

ELIMINATION 1. Tombstone Teri 2. 1580 3. 1 and 153

INDIRECT REASONING 1. a. No. No jar has a correct label. b. Red c. No. If so, the jar labeled *green* would have green jellybeans, but all labels are incorrect. d. Red - Green = Red, Red = Green, Green = Red - Green.

			3.		
2. AL	Camellia	Yellowhammer	First		Yellow
AK	Forget-Me-Not	Willow ptarmigan	Second	Liz	Purple
OK	Mistletoe	Flycatcher	Third	Joe	Green
MN	Lady's slipper	Loon	Fourth		Red

Two answers are possible. Freddie and Susie can be in either first or fourth place.

LOGICAL REASONING 1. 106 2. $1.19, 1 half dollar, 1 quarter, 4 dimes, 4 pennies 3. Rick and Jane, Lee and Marie, Bob and Jolene, Lyle and Chris 4. True, False, True, True, False

CHAPTER 2: SETS AND LOGIC

ATTRIBUTES 5. a. Each piece has 3 attributes.

b.

Attribute	Values	Attribute	Values	Attribute	Values
Size	Large Small	Shading	Plain Checkered Striped Dotted	Shape	Triangle Circle Square

6.

Sort the Pieces by	Number of Piles	Number in Each Pile
Size	2	12
Shape	3	8
Type of Shading	4	6

7. There are 24 pieces in the set. There are two ways to find the number of pieces without counting every piece: (1) multiply the number of piles for any one attribute by the number of pieces in each pile, or (2) find the product of the number of values for size, the number of values for shape, and the number of values for shading, that is, 2 x 3 x 4.

ATTRIBUTE ELIMINATION 8. Small Dotted Square 9. Large Striped Triangle 10. Large Checkered Triangle 11. Small Checkered Circle 12. Small Striped Circle since all of the other pieces are large. 13. Small Striped Square since all of the other pieces are circles. 14. There are three possible correct answers: (1) Large Striped Circle since all of the other pieces are plain. (2) Large Plain Square since all of the other pieces are circles. (3) Small Plain Circle since all of the other pieces are large.

WHAT'S DIFFERENT? 2. Depending on the train, there will either be no possible replacements or just one possible replacement. 6. Regardless of which piece is selected, 6 pieces differ from it by one attribute, 11 pieces differ from it by two attributes, and 6 pieces differ from it by three attributes. There are several correct answers for each problem 7 through 9. One answer for each is shown here.

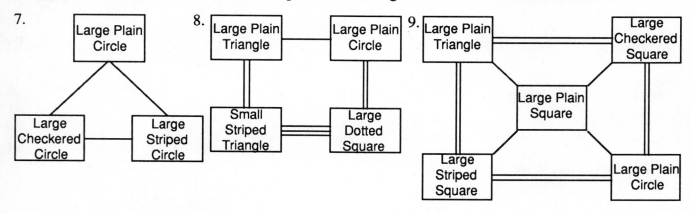

LOOPS 1. It is possible if you let the loops overlap so that the large checkered pieces can be placed in the intersection of the loops. 2. 15 pieces 3. 3 pieces 4. 3 pieces 5. 9 pieces 6. a. C b. A c. B d. D 7. There are several possible answers. Striped and Not Striped, Large and Small, or Triangle and Square are three possibilities. 8. There are several possible answers. Not Striped and Dotted or Not Circle and Triangle are two possibilities. 9. The label for the left loop is Not Square and for the right loop is Checkered. 10. a. 1 piece b. 1 piece c. 3 pieces d. 2 pieces e. 2 pieces f. 6 pieces g. 6 pieces h. 3 pieces 11. a. E b. A c. F d. G e. H f. D 12. a. Not Checkered b. Small c. Not Square

LOOPS REVISITED

13. a. Region B is the set of pieces that are square and not striped. OR
Region B is the intersection of the set of squares and the set of not striped pieces.
b. Region B = {squares}∩{not striped pieces}
14. a. Region A is the set of pieces that are not striped and not square. OR
Region A is the complement of the set of squares relative to the set of not striped pieces.
b. Region A = {not striped pieces} − {squares} OR Region A = {not striped pieces}∩{not squares}
15. a. The region inside the loops contains the pieces that are square or not striped. OR
The region inside the loops is the union of the set of squares and the set of not striped pieces.
b. The region inside the loops = {squares}∪{not striped pieces}
16. a. Region D contains the pieces that are striped and not square.
Region D is the complement of the union of the set of squares and the set of pieces that are not striped. OR Region D is the intersection of the set of pieces that are striped and the set of pieces that are not square.
b. Region D = $\overline{\{squares\}\cup\{not\ striped\ pieces\}}$ OR
Region D = {not square pieces}∩{striped pieces}

17. a. small plain triangle
large plain triangle
small checkered triangle
large checkered triangle
small dotted circle
small dotted square
small dotted triangle
large dotted circle
large dotted square
large dotted triangle
small striped triangle
large striped triangle

b. small dotted circle
small dotted triangle
small dotted square

c. small dotted circle
small dotted square
large dotted circle
large dotted square

d. small dotted triangle

e. small plain triangle
small checkered triangle
small striped triangle

f. large plain square
large plain circle
large checkered square
large checkered circle
large striped square
large striped circle

g. large plain triangle
large checkered triangle
large striped triangle

h. small dotted circle
small dotted square
large dotted circle
large dotted square

18. a. There are no pieces in the intersection. b. The intersection is empty, OR the intersection is Ø.
c. Diagram B 19. a. All of the checkered pieces are in the intersection. b. The intersection is the set of checkered pieces. c. The set of checkered pieces is a subset of the set of not striped pieces. d. Diagram A

CHAPTER 3: NUMERATION AND COMPUTATION

A VISIT TO FOURIA 2. A blue coin may be traded for four red coins, and one of the red coins traded for four white coins. 4. a. 2 blue, 3 red, 1 white b. 1 blue, 2 white c. 1 red, 3 white d. 2 red
5. a. 121_4 b. 203_4 c. 2_4 d. 23_4
6.

1_4	2_4	3_4	10_4	11_4	12_4	13_4	20_4	21_4	22_4
23_4	30_4	31_4	32_4	33_4	100_4	101_4	102_4	103_4	110_4
111_4	112_4	113_4	120_4	121_4	122_4	123_4	130_4	131_4	132_4
133_4	200_4	201_4	202_4	203_4	210_4	211_4	212_4	213_4	220_4
221_4	222_4	223_4	230_4	231_4	232_4	233_4	300_4	301_4	302_4
303_4	310_4	311_4	312_4	313_4	320_4	321_4	322_4	323_4	330_4
331_4	332_4	333_4	1000_4	1001_4	1002_4	1003_4	1010_4	1011_4	1012_4

8. a. 593_{10} b. 593

LARGEST AND SMALLEST Arrangements for the largest product (a is smallest digit, last letter is largest).

c b	d c a	e d a	f e c a
d a	e b	f c b	g d b

Arrangements for the smallest product.

b d	b d e	b d f	b d f g
a c	a c	a c e	a c e

CHAPTER 4: INTEGERS

CHARGED PARTICLES 4. a. b. c. d.

5. a. 5 b. 1 c. 2 d. 0 6. a. 15 b. 12 c. 0 7. a. 2, 2 b. 3, 3 c. 4, 4 8. a. +9 b. -7 9. 0

ADDITION AND SUBTRACTION

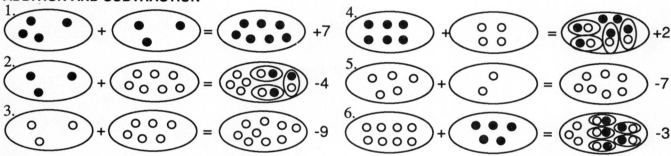

7. negative 8. The sum of two negative numbers is the negative of the sum of their absolute values.
9. a. The sum is 0 if the numbers are opposites. b. The sum is positive if the number with the larger absolute value is positive. c. The sum is negative if the number with the larger absolute value is negative. 10. Find the absolute values of the addends and subtract the smaller absolute value from the larger one. The sum is the negative of this difference if the number with the larger absolute value is negative; otherwise, the sum equals this difference.
11. Answers will vary; three possibilities are:

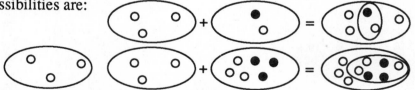

12. By adding 5 protons and 5 electrons to a set containing 2 electrons.

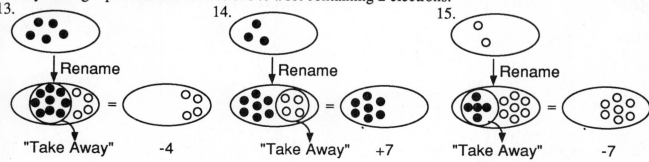

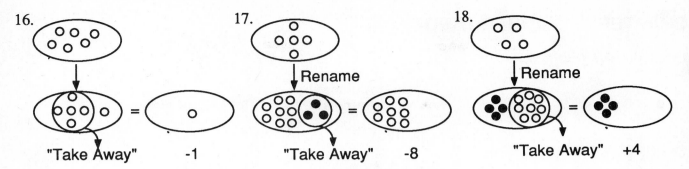

16. "Take Away" -1

17. Rename "Take Away" -8

18. Rename "Take Away" +4

19. -4 20. +7 21. -7 22. -1 23. -8 24. +4 25. They are the same.
26. If the problem in 13 through 18 is $x - y$, then the corresponding problem in 19 through 24 is $x + (-y)$.
27. To subtract an integer, add its opposite. That is, $x - y = x + (-y)$.

MULTIPLICATION AND DIVISION 1. a. +12 b. -6 c. -12 2. a. -12 b. +6 c. +12 3. a. positive b. positive c. The product is the product of the absolute values of the factors. d. negative e. The product is the negative of the product of the absolute values of the factors. 4. The product of two integers equals the product of their absolute values if both integers are positive or both are negative; otherwise the product of the two integers equals the negative of the product of their absolute values.
5. a. -3 b. -5 c. +4 6. The quotient of two integers equals the quotient of their absolute values if both integers are positive or both are negative; otherwise the quotient of the two integers equals the negative of the quotient of their absolute values.

INTEGER PATTERNS: ADDITION 1. a. If the absolute value of the positive number is greater than the absolute value of the negative number. b. If the absolute value of the two addends is the same. c. If the absolute value of the negative number is greater than the absolute value of the positive number.
2. Answers will vary. 3. Answers will vary. 4. Add the absolute values of the two numbers; the sign of the answer is negative. 5. Answers will vary.

INTEGER PATTERNS: SUBTRACTION

1.
$$4 - 0 = 4$$
$$4 - 1 = 3$$
$$4 - 2 = 2$$
$$4 - 3 = 1$$
$$4 - 4 = 0$$
$$4 - 5 = -1$$
$$4 - 6 = -2$$
$$4 - 7 = -3$$

2.
$$3 - 4 = -1$$
$$2 - 4 = -2$$
$$1 - 4 = -3$$
$$0 - 4 = -4$$
$$-1 - 4 = -5$$
$$-2 - 4 = -6$$
$$-3 - 4 = -7$$
$$-4 - 4 = -8$$

3.
$$4 - 3 = 1$$
$$4 - 2 = 2$$
$$4 - 1 = 3$$
$$4 - 0 = 4$$
$$4 - -1 = 5$$
$$4 - -2 = 6$$
$$4 - -3 = 7$$

4.
$$-4 - 3 = -7$$
$$-4 - 2 = -6$$
$$-4 - 1 = -5$$
$$-4 - 0 = -4$$
$$-4 - -1 = -3$$
$$-4 - -2 = -2$$
$$-4 - -3 = -1$$

6. For any two integers a and b, $a - b = a + (-b)$.

INTEGER PATTERNS: MULTIPLICATION AND DIVISION 1. a. Second factors decrease by one.
b. Products decrease by four. 2. The product of a negative number and a positive number is negative.
3. a. The second factors decrease by one. b. The products increase by three. 4. The product of two negative numbers is positive. 5. a. $-12 \div 4 = -3$, and $-12 \div -3 = 4$. b. The quotient of a positive number and a negative number is negative; the quotient of two negative numbers is positive.

CHAPTER 5: NUMBER THEORY

THE SQUARE EXPERIMENT

TABLE 1

No. of Squares	Dimensions of the Rectangular Arrays	Total No. of Arrays
1	1 x 1	1
2	1 x 2, 2 x 1	2
3	1 x 3, 3 x 1	2
4	1 x 4, 4 x 1, 2 x 2	3
5	1 x 5, 5 x 1	2
6	1 x 6, 6 x 1, 2 x 3, 3 x 2	4
7	1 x 7, 7 x 1	2
8	1 x 8, 8 x 1, 2 x 4, 4 x 2	4
9	1 x 9, 9 x 1, 3 x 3	3
10	1 x 10, 10 x 1, 2 x 5, 5 x 2	4
11	1 x 11, 11 x 1	2
12	1 x 12, 12 x 1, 2 x 6, 6 x 2, 3 x 4, 4 x 3	6
13	1 x 13, 13 x 1	2
14	1 x 14, 14 x 1, 2 x 7, 7 x 2	4

TABLE 2

A	B	C	D
Only One Array	Only Two Arrays	More Than Two Arrays	An Odd Number of Arrays
1	2,3,5,7,11,13,...	4,6,8,9,10, 12,14,...	1,4,9,16,...

2. a. 8 b. C c. 1, 2, 3, 4, 6, 8, 12, 24 3. a. 1, 2, 4, 8, 16 b. 5 c. C, D 4. The number of factors is equal to the number of arrays. 5. a. The numbers in column D are square numbers; when a square is rotated from horizontal to vertical, the dimensions remain the same. b. 25, 36, 49 6. a. Prime b. Composite c. Square 7. Composite numbers and all square numbers except 1; they have more than 2 factors. 8. No 9. D-{1} 10. B ∪ C 11. Ø 12. A 13. A 14. C ∪ {1}

INTERESTING NUMBERS When the digits of **13** are reversed, the number formed, 31, is also a prime number. **64** is also a perfect square. **69** is still 69 when read upside down, that is, 69 has point symmetry. **121** is a palindrome, that is, its value is unchanged when its digits are reversed.
1. Answers will vary; 1, 8, and 27 are possiblities. 2. Answers will vary; 1, 4, and 9 are possibilities.
3. Answers will vary; 2, 3, and 7 are possiblities. 4. Answers will vary; 292, 8338, and 757 are possibilities. 5. Answers will vary, 17, 37, and 79 are possiblities. 6. 5 (101, 131, 151, 181, 191)
7. 8 if single digit numbers are considered to be palindromes; otherwise 343.
9.

Number	Rating	Number	Rating	Number	Rating	Number	Rating
576	35	756	31	864	31	936	31
672	31	780	31	900	37	960	35
720	33	792	31	924	31	990	31
729	30	840	35				

10. 23 if the sum of the digits is greater than 14. 11. a. 10 points for being a perfect cube, 7 for being a perfect square, 2 for being odd, and 1 for each of the following factors: $1, n, \sqrt{n}, \sqrt[3]{n},$ and $\left(\sqrt[3]{n}\right)^2$.

b. $729 = 9 \times 9 \times 9$ c. 30 12. 900 Interest Rating = 37

NUMBER OF FACTORS 13. $5 = 5^1$, $24 = 2^3 \times 3^1$, $2^2 \times 5^2 = 100$, $2^4 \times 5^1 = 80$, $60 = 2^2 \times 3^1 \times 5^1$, $72 = 2^3 \times 3^2$ 15. The number of factors is one more than the exponent. 16. a. 2^4, 3^4, etc. b. 2^6, 3^6, etc. c. 2^{10}, 3^{10}, etc. 17. To find the number of factors, add 1 to each of the exponents in the prime factorization, and find the product of the sums. [Example: $20 = 2^2 \times 5^1$; number of factors = $(2 + 1) \times (1 + 1) = 6$] 18. yes [Example: $100 = 2^2 \times 5^2$ and $(2 + 1) \times (2 + 1) = 9$. 1, 2, 4, 5, 10, 20, 25, 50, and 100 are factors.] 19. $2^3 \times 3^2 \times 5^1$ 20. $(3 + 1) \times (2 + 1) \times (1 + 1) = 4 \times 3 \times 2 = 24$; the factors are 1, 2, 3, 4, 5, 6, 8, 9, 10, 12, 15, 18, 20, 24, 30, 36, 40, 45, 60, 72, 90, 120, 180, 360 21. To find the total number of factors of a number, add 1 to each of the exponents in the prime factorization of the number, and find the product of the sums. 22. $45360 = 2^4 \times 3^4 \times 5^1 \times 7^1$

POOL FACTORS See KEY IDEAS and EXTENSIONS sections on pages 63 and 64.

CHAPTER 6: RATIONAL NUMBERS

SQUARE FRACTIONS 1. Isosceles right triangles 2. Congruent 3. 1/2, the two triangles make up the square. 4. Isosceles right triangles 5. Equal 6. 1/2 7. 1/4 8. a. Figure 3, right isosceles triangle b. Figure B, isosceles tapezoid 9. a. similar b. similar 10. a. 1/2 b. 1/4 c. 1/8 d. 1/3 11. a. Figure C, trapezoid b. Figure 4, isosceles right triangle 12. a. similar b. similar c. similar 13. a. 1/2 b. 1/4 c. 1/8 d. 1/5 e. 1/6 f. 1/16 14. a. Figure 5, square b. Figure D, trapezoid 15. a. 2/5 b. 2/1 c. 1/1 d. 1/3 e. 2/3 f. 1/2 g. 1/4 h. 1/8 16. a. 5/3 b. 5/2 c. 5/4 d. 5/16 17. Answers will vary. 18. a. Figure 6, right isosceles triangle b. Figure 7, parallelogram 19. a. 1/3 b. 1/8 c. 1/5 d. 1/2 e. 1/2 f. 1/6 g. 1/2 h. 1/6 20. a. 3/5 b. 3/2 c. 1/2 d. 3/4 21. a. 2/3 b. 1/2 c. 2/1 d. 1/1 e. 1/1 f. 1/3 g. 1/4 h. 1/8 i. 2/5

PEOPLE PROPORTIONS 1. Wing span/Height will be close to 1/1. 2. Comparisons of the ratios will be difficult due to disparity of the numbers in the fractions. 3. Each of the individual ratios (Wing span/Height, Tibia/Height, etc.) should be nearly the same for all persons measured. 4. Wing span/Height is about 1/1, Wrist/Neck is about 1/2. 5. Tibia is about 1/4 height, radius is about 1/6 height. 6. Navel to floor/Height is about 0.618, Height/Navel to floor is about 1.618 7. Answers will vary. 8. 1.618034. The decimal portions of the two numbers are the same. 9. Answers will vary.

POPULATION STUDIES 1. Calif. 65.13, Mont. 2.19, N. J. 390.96, Brazil 16.84, H. K. 5528.61, Japan 326.74, U. S. 26.28 2. a. 147,222,460 people b. 61.09% 3. a. 42,427 people b. It would be about the same as that of a small city. 4. 365.27 people/sq km 5. a. 180.88 sq m b. 13.45 m c. probably about the same 6. a. 30.5 years b. 39 years c. 21.5 years

CHAPTER 7: DECIMALS AND PERCENTS

DECIMAL PATTERNS 1. a. $0.\overline{1}$ b. $0.\overline{3}$ c. $0.\overline{6}$ d. $0.\overline{4}$ e. $0.\overline{8}$ f. $0.\overline{5}$ 2. a. 1 b. 1 c. The numerator is the repeating block in the decimal equivalent of the fraction. 3. a. $0.\overline{2}$ b. $0.\overline{7}$ c. $0.\overline{9}$ 4. $0.\overline{9}$ 5. 1 6. $1 = 0.\overline{9}$ 7. a. 0.1 b. 0.01 c. 0.001 d. 0.5 e. 0.13 f. 0.577 8. a. $0.\overline{13}$ b. $0.\overline{16}$ c. $0.\overline{05}$ d. $0.\overline{47}$ e. $0.\overline{78}$ f. $0.\overline{36}$ 9. a. 2 b. 2 c. If the numerator contains two digits, the numerator is the repeating block. Otherwise, the repeating block is 0 followed by the numerator. 10. a. $0.\overline{213}$ b. $0.\overline{783}$ c. $0.\overline{2435}$ d. $0.\overline{0059}$ e. $0.\overline{52063}$ f. $0.\overline{02451}$ 11. The decimal equivalent is a repeating decimal in which there are no digits between the decimal and the repeating block and the length of the repeating block is equal to the number of 9's in the denominator. The repeating block is n zeros followed by the numerator of the fraction where n = the length of the denominator - the length of the numerator. 12. Convert the fraction to a mixed number. The decimal equivalent is the whole number part of the mixed number plus decimal equivalent of the fractional part. The decimal equivalent of the fraction can be found using the rule in problem 11.

13. $\dfrac{23}{90} = \dfrac{23}{9} \times \dfrac{1}{10} = 2\dfrac{5}{9} \times \dfrac{1}{10} = 2.\overline{5} \times 0.1 = 0.2\overline{5}$

14. a. $0.2\overline{1}$ b. $0.7\overline{4}$ c. $0.64\overline{7}$ d. $0.0\overline{28}$ e. $0.99\overline{7}$ f. $0.28\overline{13}$

REPEATING DECIMALS

2/3	$0.\overline{6}$	Repeats	3	1	0
29/90	$0.3\overline{2}$	Repeats	$2 \times 3^2 \times 5$	1	1
17/99	$0.\overline{17}$	Repeats	$3^2 \times 11$	2	0
19/3500	$0.005\overline{428571}$	Repeats	$2^2 \times 5^3 \times 7$	6	3
17/200	0.085	Terminates	$2^3 \times 5^2$	0	3
1/6	$0.1\overline{6}$	Repeats	2×3	1	1
1/8	0.125	Terminates	2^3	0	3
7/15	$0.4\overline{6}$	Repeats	3×5	1	1
3/125	0.024	Terminates	5^3	0	3
1/140	$0.00\overline{714285}$	Repeats	$2^2 \times 5 \times 7$	6	2
3/100	0.03	Terminates	$2^2 \times 5^2$	0	2
17/400	0.0425	Terminates	$2^4 \times 5^2$	0	4
119/5000	0.0238	Terminates	$2^3 \times 5^4$	0	4
4179/4950	$0.844\overline{2}$	Repeats	$2 \times 3^3 \times 5^2 \times 11$	2	2
1/7	$0.\overline{142857}$	Repeats	7	6	0
99/260	$0.3\overline{80769230}$	Repeats	$2^2 \times 5 \times 13$	6	2
2/35	$0.0\overline{571428}$	Repeats	5×7	6	1
7/20	0.35	Terminates	$2^2 \times 5$	0	2
5/24	$0.208\overline{3}$	Repeats	$2^3 \times 3$	1	3
121/600	$0.201\overline{6}$	Repeats	$2^3 \times 3 \times 5^2$	1	3

15. a. 2 and 5 b. no c. The decimal equivalent terminates if and only if the only prime factors of the denominator of the fraction are 2 and/or 5. 16. a. The number of digits between the decimal point and the beginning of the repeating block is the maximum of the exponents of 2 and/or 5 in the prime factorization of the denominator. b. yes c. same answer as part a

FLEX-IT 1 - 4. Answers will vary.

CHAPTER 8: PROBABILITY

WHAT'S THE MESSAGE?   2. b. Fifty trials probably is not enough to obtain an accurate estimate of the probability. 3. We assumed that 50 trials will be sufficient to get an accurate estimate of the probability, and that the probability of transmitting an erroneous data bit is independent of the results of the previous transmissions. 4. The advantage is that the probability of translating a message bit incorrectly is reduced. The disadvantage is that it takes three times as long to transmit a message. 5. 0.028 7. by conducting more trials

AN AIRLINE'S DILEMMA 1. 126 reservations 2. Roll the die one time. Let the numbers 1-5 mean the passenger shows up. 3. A trial consists of rolling the die 126 times, once for each person holding a reservation. 4. The observation of interest is how many times one of the digits 1-5 appears in a trial. If this happens less than 105 times, then you get a seat on the flight. 11. The free ticket is for a round trip to any destination so it includes fares for more than one flight.

THE LAW OF AVERAGES 15. 7 17. The length of the longest string increases. 18. You really can't conclude anything. The probabilities show a great deal of variation. 5. The probabilities get close to 0.028. 20. No, the difference can get larger. 21. a. They will vary greatly from day to day. b. The ratio approaches 1. c. Not necessarily. Problem 20 shows that they can get further apart. d. The first part of the statement is correct, but the conclusion is incorrect. 22. a. No, in a small number of trials it is not unusual to have the actual number of outcomes differ greatly from the expected number. b. No, as the number of trials increases, it becomes more likely that you will encounter long strings of heads or tails. c. 0.5

CHAPTER 9: EXPLORING DATA

WHAT'S THE AVERAGE? 1. a. Hawaii or Oregon b. 6 2. 5 3. about 6 (6 1/9) 4. 6 5. 5 6. about 7 (6.8) 7. The median and the mode were unchanged, but the mean increased significantly. The length of 13 letters is very large in comparison to the other lengths. The mean of a set of data may, as this example shows, be greatly affected by very large or very small data points. 8. 6.5 9. 8 10. 6.5 (6 7/12) 11. All three averages were increased by these additions. The mean and the median increased about the same amount. The mode was affected the most, even though 8 occurred only one more time than 5. The mean always tends toward the mode whereas the median may either be moved toward the mode or away from it depending on whether the mode is above (as in this case) or below the center of the data. 12. To compute the mean, add the lengths of the names and divide the total by n. 13. a. Mode. It is likely that one shoe size would be sold with a higher frequency than the others. This would affect both the median and the mean. b. Mean. Household sizes tend to fall in a narrow range and no single size occurs with a significantly greater frequency than the others. c. Median. The mean would be greatly affected by very high or very low incomes, and it is unlikely that there is a single income that occurs with an unusually high frequency that would affect the median. 14. a. Mean, because the .495 batting average makes it largest b. Mode, because it is the smallest average c. Median, because .495 is unusually large in comparison to the rest of the data (thus the mean would not accurately reflect the data) and 2 out of 5 is not an unusually high frequency for the mode

STATISTICS WITH "M&M'S"® 6. No, you would need a larger sample to make an accurate prediction. 9. a. Maximum and minimum values, clusters and gaps in the data, outliers, the median, and modes may all be easily identified from a line plot. b. The same information may be obtained from a frequency table; however, clusters and gaps in the data and outliers may not be as easy to spot. 10. Bar graphs are usually easier to construct and to read. The reason is that it is difficult to accurately divide the picture being used into fractional parts and to recognize the parts. 13. The manufacturer could use the results to determine the ideal proportion of each color "M&M's"® to include in the bags. The manufacturer probably would not use the data, however, since it was not obtained from a random sample.

THE WEATHER REPORT

1.
SAN FRANCISCO		WICHITA	
6	1 1 2 3 4	8	0 1
5	2 3 5 5 8	7	1 6
4	9 9	6	6
		5	6 9
		4	4 4
		3	0 4 5

2.
	SF	WICHITA
Mean	56.8	56.3
Median	56.5	57.5
Mode	49,55,61	44

6. 2 months 7. The line graph 8. The mean and median temperatures are about the same, but the range of the temperatures varies widely. 9. The mean or median temperature does not accurately describe the annual temperature for Wichita since the range is so large; the mean or median does accurately describe the climate in San Francisco since the range is only 15 degrees. 10. Range of data 11. a. 37.46

b. 37.41 c. San Francisco 12. San Francisco is on the coast so the climate is moderated by the Pacific Ocean currents.
13. .   **PORTLAND, ME**   **PORTLAND, OR**

8 7 2	6	3 3 7 8
9 3	5	0 4 7
8 3	4	1 3 6 6
8 2	3	9
6 3 2	2	

14. Latitude for Portland, OR is 45.31, Mean = 53.1, Median = 52, Mode = 63 and 46; latitude for Portland, ME is 43.39, Mean = 45.1, Median = 45.5, there is no mode.

CHAPTER 10 : INTRODUCTION TO GEOMETRY

CLASSIFYING TRIANGLES 1. B,E,F,G,I,L,M,N 2. D,E,H,I,J,L 3. A,F,G,K 4. H,D
 5. A,C,D,H,J,K 6. B,C,M,N 7. a. No b. No 8. Scalene-acute, scalene-right, scalene-obtuse, isosceles-acute, isosceles-right, isosceles-obtuse, equilateral-acute 9. equilateral-right, equilateral-obtuse

CLASSIFYING QUADRILATERALS   1. A,B,E,L,M 2. C,G,N 3. B,F,I,H,L 4. B,F,G,I,L
 5. A,B,E,F,I,K,L,M 6. A,B,E,F,I,K,L,M 7. A,B,E,F,I,K,L,M 8. B,D,E,J,L,M 9. A,B,E,F,I,K,L,M
10. B,D,E,F,G,I,L,M 11. B,E,L,M 12. B,E,D,G,L,M 13. B,L 14. B,F,I,L 15. A,B,E,F,I,K,L,M
16. C,G,N 17. B,E,L,M 18. D 19. 3,4,5,6,7,9,10 20. 1,3,4,5,6,7,8,9,10,11,12 21. 5,6,7,9
22. 1,5,6,7,8,9,10,11,12 23. 2 24. 8,10,12 25. A square is a quadrilateral with all sides congruent and one right angle. 26. A parallelogram is a quadrilateral with opposite sides parallel. 27. A rectangle is a quadrilateral with opposite sides parallel and one right angle. 28. A trapezoid is a quadrilateral with one pair of parallel sides. 29. A rhombus is a quadrilateral with four equal sides 30. See 31.

31.

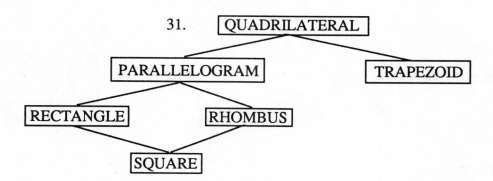

TRIANGLE PROPERTIES 1. The triangles are different. 2. an infinite number 9. a. 6 and 8 b. The sum is less than or equal to the length of the longest side. 10. a. 3, 4, 5, and 7 b. The sum is greater than the length of the longest side. 13. The sum of the lengths of any two sides is greater than the length of the third side. 14. a. 3 - acute scalene, 4 - acute isosceles, 5 - equilateral, 7 - obtuse scalene b. The triangles for each exercise have exactly the same shape and size.

Problem	Sum of the Given Angles	Is a Triangle Possible?	If Yes, What Is the Measure of the Third Angle?
15	80°	yes	100°
16	90°	yes	90°
17	185°	no	
18	120°	yes	60°
19	180°	no	
20	160°	yes	20°

21. a. The sum is greater than or equal to 180°. b. The sum is less than 180°. 24. The sum of the measures of the angles of a triangle is 180°. 25. a. 15 - obtuse scalene, 16 - right scalene, 18 - equilateral, 20 - acute isosceles b. The triangles have the same shape but different sizes. d. The corresponding ratios are equal.

TO BE OR NOT TO BE CONGRUENT? 4. a. The angle is included by the sides. b. The triangles are congruent. c. If two sides and the included angle of one triangle are congruent to two sides and the included angle of another triangle, then the triangles are congruent. 8. a. The side is included by the angles. b. The triangles are congruent. c. If two angles and the included side of one triangle are congruent to two angles and the included side of another triangle, then the triangles are congruent. 9. a. The side is opposite one of the angles. c. The triangles are congruent. d. If two angles and a side of one triangle are congruent to the corresponding parts in another triangle, then the triangles are congruent. 13. a. The angle is opposite one of the sides. b. 12 c. 10 d. a right triangle e. If you know two sides and the angle opposite one of them, then it is possible to have a unique right triangle, two different triangles, or no triangle.

CHAPTER 11: CONGRUENCE AND SIMILARITY

A PROBLEM OF PERSPECTIVE 1. e. YA:IS = 1.56 YA:OE = 1.56 IS:OE = 1.00
2. a. Quadrilateral PYRA is similar to quadrilateral MIDS because the corresponding angles are congruent and the ratio of the lengths of corresponding sides is constant. b. Quadrilateral PYRA is similar to quadrilateral CONE because the corresponding angles are congruent and the ratio of the lengths of corresponding sides is constant. c. Quadrilateral CONE is congruent to quadrilateral MIDS because the measures of the corresponding sides and the corresponding angles are equal. 3. a. 1.56 b. 1.56 c. 1.56 d. They are equal to the ratio of the corresponding sides of quadrilaterals PYRA and MIDS. 4. a. They appear to be parallel. b. Like the horizon, nothing can be seen that is beyond this line. c. As objects move toward these points along the perspective lines, the objects get smaller and smaller until they disappear completely at the vanishing point. d. Because objects whose corresponding points lie on lines drawn through these points are similar. 5. a. 1.56 b. 1.56 c. 1.56 d. They are equal to the ratio of the corresponding sides of quadrilaterals PYRA and CONE. e. Because the objects whose verticies correspond to these points are similar.

DILATIONS 6. a. Yes, the corresponding angles are congruent. b. 2:1 c. 2:1 7. a. They are congruent. b. △STR is congruent to △ABC. c. The area of △A'B'C' is 4 times the area of △ABC. 8. a. Yes, the corresponding angles are congruent. b. 3:1 c. 3:1 9. a. yes b. 3:2 c. 3:2 d. The area of △A"B"C" is 9/4 times the area of △A'B'C'. 10. a. yes b. 2:1 c. 2:1 d. The area of

$\triangle XYZ$ is 4 times the area of $\triangle ABC$. e. It changes the position of the image. 11. a. J'M : JM b. The area of $\triangle J'K'L'$ is $(J'M'/JM)^2$ times the area of $\triangle JKL$.

OUTDOOR GEOMETRY 1. $\angle DAN = \angle JIM$ and $\angle NDA = \angle MJI$ 2. NA/DA = MI/JI 3. $\angle JAM = \angle EIM$ and $\angle JMA = \angle EMI$ 4. JA/AM = EI/IM 5. $\angle EDC = \angle BAF$ and $\angle DCE = \angle ABF$ 6. ED/DC = AF/BA 7. Add the measure of the distance from the eye to the ground to DE. 8. $\angle LIN = \angle NDA$ and $\angle ILN = \angle DAN$ 9. LI/IN = DA/DN

CHAPTER 12: TRANSFORMATIONAL GEOMETRY

REFLECTIONS 3. a. The segments are perpendicular to the line. b. S is a point on the line. c. S and S' are the same point.

REFLECTIONS REVISITED 7. a. The measure of an angle and its reflection are equal. b. The length of a segment and its reflection are equal. 8. congruent 9. a. counterclockwise b. clockwise c. It reverses orientation.

TRANSLATIONS 1. d. no e. The "tracks" appear to be parallel and congruent. 2. b. 4.4 cm c. They are twice as long. d. in the direction from ℓ_3 to ℓ_4 (to the right) 3. b. They are twice as long. c. in the direction from ℓ_4 to ℓ_3 (to the left) 4. a. 2x b. The direction of motion is parallel to the direction line ℓ_5 must be moved to make it coincide with line ℓ_6. 5. All of the properties are preserved by a translation.

ROTATIONS 1. 70° 2. a. 140° b. twice as large c. clockwise 3. a. 140°; twice as large b. counterclockwise 4. a. R and X are on the circle with radius KA. S and Y are on the circle with radius KB. P and Z are on the circle with radius KC. b. no 5. a. 2x degrees b. The direction of rotation is clockwise (counterclockwise) if line ℓ_3 can be made to coincide with line ℓ_4 by rotating it clockwise (counterclockwise) through an acute angle. 6. All of the properties are preserved by a rotation.

GLIDE REFLECTIONS 1. The midpoints all lie on the reflecting line. 3. a translation 4. a. translation b. rotation c. reflection d. reflection e. glide reflection 5. a. glide reflection or rotation b. rotation c. rotation d. rotation e. reflection f. translation

CHAPTER 13: PERIMETER AND AREA

PICK'S THEOREM

Number of Points on the Perimeter	3	4	5	6	7	8	9	10
Area of the Polygon	1/2	1	3/2	2	5/2	3	7/2	4

2. $A = 1/2\, N_p - 1$

PICK'S THEOREM REVISITED 4. $A = 1/2\, N_p - 1 + N_i$

RIGHT OR NOT?

TABLE 1	(SAMPLE ENTRIES)					TABLE 2	(SAMPLE ENTRIES)				
100	36	64	100	right		10	100	6	8	100	right
36	16	25	41	acute		6	36	4	5	41	acute
169	81	100	181	acute		11	121	5	8	89	obtuse
121	25	64	89	obtuse							

3. a. acute b. right c. obtuse

CHAPTER 14: COORDINATE GEOMETRY

MYSTERIOUS MIDPOINTS 2. Each quadrilateral is a parallelogram. 3. Answers will vary.
5. a. Yes. In 4a, the figure formed is a parallelogram; in 4b, a rectangle; in 4c, a rhombus; and in 4d, a square. 5. b. Yes, the square 6. Each quadrilateral WXYZ is the same as the original quadrilateral in problem 4. 7. a. parallelogram b. rhombus c. rectangle d. square. 8. Answers will vary.

RECTANGLES AND CURVES

TABLE 1

b	1	2	3	4	6	9	12	18	36
h	36	18	12	9	6	4	3	2	1
P	74	40	30	26	24	26	30	40	74

3. Yes (Example: 3.6 x 10) 4. Infinite 5. Answers will vary. 6. No. Answers will vary with the placement of the points. 7. No. The base and height cannot have a value of zero. 8. No. The height cannot have a negative value. 9. 36 10. 24 11. 6 x 6. 12. No. The base can be extended to any length as the height approaches zero. 13. $A = b \times h = 36$. Since the base can be extended to any length, there is no maximum perimeter. 14. A rubber band that would stretch without breaking.

TABLE 2

b	1	2	3	4	5	6	7	8	9	10	11
h	11	10	9	8	7	6	5	4	3	2	1
A	11	20	27	32	35	36	35	32	27	20	11

16. No 17. (12,0) Since $P = 2 \times b + 2 \times h$, if $b = 12$, then $2 \times b = 24$, and $h = 0$, therefore there is no rectangle. 18. b is approximately 2.6 19. 36 20. 6 x 6 21. No. Since the measures of a side must be greater than zero, the area must be greater than zero, but there is no minimum value.
22. b approaches 12

CENTIMETER SQUARE DOT GRID

CENTIMETER SQUARE DOT GRID

CENTIMETER SQUARE DOT GRID

CENTIMETER SQUARE DOT GRID

CENTIMETER GRAPH GRID

CENTIMETER GRAPH GRID

CENTIMETER GRAPH GRID

CENTIMETER GRAPH GRID

CENTIMETER TRIANGULAR DOT GRID

CENTIMETER TRIANGULAR DOT GRID

CENTIMETER TRIANGULAR DOT GRID

NOTES

NOTES

NOTES